Scholastic Guides

Putting It In Writing

Scholastic Guides
Putting It In Writing

Steve Otfinoski

Scholastic
Reference

Scholastic Inc.

NEW YORK   TORONTO   LONDON   AUCKLAND   SYDNEY

Illustrations by Peter Spacek

Scholastic would like to thank the following schools and people: Babylon Grade School:
Jennifer Brehm, Alexandra Brucculeri, Catherine Carbonaro, Mr. Feinstein, Dr. Esther Fusco,
Mrs. Ierardi, Elisabeth Kiernan, Mrs. Marrow, Ms. Mastrandrea, Mrs. Ricchuiti, Tim Ruggeri,
Erica Sterling / Bank Street School for Children: Amanda Altman / Bleyl Junior High:
R. Katie Barnes / Columbia Middle School: Sam Elliot, Ben Felton, Peter Klein, Jessica Parker
/ Gillespie Elementary School: Brian White / The Lab School at P.S. 198: Benjamin Pred /
Stratford Academy: Ms. Paige's and Mrs. Stolzenberg's Fourth, Fifth, and Sixth Grades in
the Advanced Learning Program; Toby Anekwe; Cara Bertini; Jay Bertini; Adam Dinihanian;
Lisa Donofrio; John Duggan; Thomas Henthorn; Jasmine Hromjak; Sarah Jacobs; David
Mencel; Michael Mendez; Luke Meyer; Daniel Otfinoski; Jeremy Prentiss; Gregory Trupp;
Jonathan Warner. Illustrations by Peter Spacek.

ISBN 0-590-49459-7

23 22 21 20   01 02 03

Printed in the U.S.A.   09

Contents

Introduction

Letters

Reports

LIST OF EXAMPLES

Writing gives us a focused way to share our knowledge, thoughts and feelings. Unlike speaking, which is often informal, writing has forms that signal to a reader the purpose of what you are saying. For example, when you invite someone to a party, you don't send along an essay on the importance of birthdays. But if you include the time, date, and place, your friends and family will clearly understand the importance of your birthday!

Putting It In Writing shows you different ways to organize your ideas to help you get the results that you want — information for a school paper, a visit from an out-of-town friend, even better grades. Along with the explanation for each form of writing, there are samples. Many of these samples were written by kids your age.

These samples are not meant to be copied or even imitated, but they can give you ideas about what kinds of information to include in your own writing. Once you know the key points to include in your letter or report, you can use your own style to express yourself.

Because this is a reference book, you don't have to read it from cover to cover. You can use the Table of Contents at the front and the Index at the back to look up the kind of writing you're going to do.

Don't worry if your first efforts are less than perfect. Good writing takes effort and practice. But if you follow the information, hints, and samples in this book, putting it in writing can be fun, too.

Business Letters

Business letters aren't just written by business people. Anytime you send for information for a school assignment, need to complain about something you bought, or want to express your opinion in a newspaper or magazine, you will be writing a business letter.

Three Business Letter Formats

◀ • **The block format.** In this format all parts of the letter run along the left side of the page (margin). No paragraphs in the body are indented, but an extra space is left between paragraphs.

◀ • **The modified block format.** In this format the heading and the closing and signature run along the right margin. All the other parts run along the left margin.

◀ • **The semiblock format.** This format is the same as the block format, except that the paragraphs in the body are indented.

In the sample letters in this chapter, we will use the block format.

Six Parts of a Business Letter
· ·

▶ Heading

SEE ALSO
State
Abbreviations,
p.132

The heading consists of your address and the date.

> 502 Elm Street
> Topeka, KS 66608
> January 24, 1994

The heading appears about an inch from the top of the page in the top right or left corner, depending on the letter format used.

2 Inside Address

The **inside address** consists of the name and address of the person to whom you are writing. It usually appears four lines below the heading, and it is always at the left margin.

Here are some tips for writing the inside address:

✐ It is up to you whether or not you include Mr., Ms., Dr., etc. before the name. However, if the person holds a high public office, such as U.S. Senator or Representative, the words **The Most Honorable** must precede his or her name. Christian religious figures are often addressed with a "the" in an address. For example, **The Reverend**.

✐ If the person has a title (Vice-President, Editor), it should be included after the name, either on the same line (separated by a comma) or on the next line.

✐ If the letter is being sent to the person's work place, the name of the company or business should be included on a separate line.

> Philip Grabowski, Program Director
> The Kid Channel
> 1409 Colonial Blvd.
> Philadelphia, PA 19056

---

3 Salutation

The most traditional **salutation**, or greeting, for a business letter is **Dear** followed by the word **Mr., Ms., Mrs.,** or **Miss.** This is followed by the person's last name and a colon. All the words in a salutation should begin with capital letters.

> Dear Ms. Jones:
> Dear Mrs. Lowe:

If you are writing to a company rather than a specific person or position, use one of these other salutations:

To Whom It May Concern:

Dear Sir or Madam:

Dear Ladies and Gentlemen:

Special Salutations

Here are some special salutations for professional people or elected officials:

for a religious leader	→	**Dear Rabbi Cohen** (The Reverend Matthew Jamison becomes Dear Mr. Jamison or Father Jamison)
for a college professor	→	**Dear Professor Cook**
for a medical doctor	→	**Dear Dr. Sharp**
for a U.S. Representative	→	**Dear Ms. Ricci**
for a U.S. Senator	→	**Dear Senator Goldfarb**
for the President of the United States	→	**Dear Mr. President** or **Dear President Clinton**

Notice that **Professor**, **Senator**, **President**, **Father** and **Rabbi** are spelled out in full.

▶ Body

The **body** is the main part of the letter where you write what you have to say to the person. Skip one line after the salutation, and begin. Generally, begin the body of a business letter with a brief personal greeting, then state your business, and end with a thank-you (if necessary).

✐ **Get to the point**. After a brief greeting, get down to business. Don't waste time in small talk.

✐ **Don't use slang, and try to avoid contractions.** Business letters are usually formal. Increase your chances of making a good impression by using standard English.

✐ **Even though it's a business letter, don't be too formal.** You still want to sound like you.

5 ▶ Closing

The closing is the ending to your letter. In the block format, the closing appears in the bottom left corner of the letter, directly under the body.

Only the first word in a closing should be capitalized. It is always followed by a comma. Here are some typical closings:

- **Truly yours** and **Yours truly** are the most common closings in a business letter.

- **Sincerely** and **Sincerely yours** are less formal and better to use if you know the person.

- **Respectfully yours** is used only for important officials.

Yours truly,

Don Alan

6 ▶ Signature

The signature is your full name, signed. Your signature should appear directly below the closing. It should always be written in ink. Below it, write your name in block letters (or type it four lines below the closing, if you're using a typewriter or computer). This way, if the reader can't read your signature, he or she will still be able to read your name.

Writing a Draft

It's a good idea to write a first draft (a practice version) of your letter. This way you can catch any mistakes or errors, check the content, and write the letter again neatly. You will also be able to save the draft copy for your records.

Samples of Business Letters

Asking for Information

SEE ALSO
Writing
Social Studies
Reports,
p.100
Appendix
Where to Write
for State
Information,
p.133

Here are some cases where you might need to write for information:

- You need to know something for a research report.

- You're interviewing someone for a report.

- You're going on a vacation and want information from the state or country you plan to visit.

- You're curious about something and want to know more.

Here are some tips to keep in mind:

T I P S

- ✎ **Be specific.** Ask for the specific information you need. It will make it easier for the person to answer.

- ✎ **State the purpose of your request.** Tell why you need this information — for a school assignment or some other important reason. You'll be more likely to get the information.

✐ **Be polite and pleasant.** The person is probably going out of his or her way to help you, and taking time from other tasks. Make sure you thank the person.

Here are two letters asking for information:

47 Field Road
Jamestown, NC 27282
December 14, 1994

Heading

California Office of Tourism
1121 L Street, Suite 103
Sacramento, CA   95814

Inside address

To Whom It May Concern:

Salutation

In school we are studying the United States. We all chose a state to gather information about. Since I chose California, I am writing to you. Please send me a brochure and information.

Purpose of request

Thank you for your help.

Thank-you

Yours truly,

Closing

Cara Bertini

Signature

Cara Bertini

563 Jefferson Blvd.
Rutherford, CT 07074
May 22, 1995

Department of Industry and Trade
P.O. Box 1776
Atlanta, GA 30301

To Whom It May Concern:

I would like a brochure about Georgia with a road map and tourist attractions. My class wants to learn more about your state.

Additional request

I would also like some information on the Olympic Games, which will be held in Atlanta in 1996. Please send it to me as soon as possible. Thank you.

Sincerely,

Luke Meyer

Luke Meyer

Inviting a Guest Speaker

Sometimes your class may invite a guest to come to speak to you about a subject or place you are studying. This person may be someone you know or a stranger who is an expert on this subject.

These letters are more friendly and personal than the ones to the tourist boards.

Here are two letters asking for a personal visit:

975 Yale Ave.
Minot, ND 58701
March 9, 1994

Mrs. Diana Danforth
222 Cannon Crossing
Bismarck, ND 58501

Dear Mrs. Danforth:

Hello. Our class is learning about Greece in our Social Studies unit. We wondered if you could come in and talk to us about it. We figured you would know a lot about this country because you have traveled there before.

Request stated

We know from other times when you shared your knowledge of foreign countries with us that it's interesting and helpful. Believe me, our class would really enjoy it if you would tell us about what you know about Greece. Please take this into consideration.

Appreciation of previous visits

Thank you!

Sincerely yours,

Lisa Donofrio

Lisa Donofrio

P.S. How are you? We miss you <u>a lot!</u> Bye!

SEE ALSO
Friendly Letters
Postscript,
p.35

338 Ranch Road
Minot, ND 58701
March 12, 1994

Ms. Diana Danforth
222 Cannon Crossing
Bismarck, ND 58501

Dear Ms. Danforth:

I have heard that you have been to Greece. In our Greece unit we have been learning about the ancient civilizations.

Since you have been to Greece, I would like to know if you have seen the ancient ruins. We have learned a lot from a textbook, but a personal experience would be a lot better. Your knowledge of Greece can help the whole class. I would like you to come and share your experiences with everyone.

I hope that you think about my request and come visit our class.

Sincerely,

Jeremy Prentiss

Jeremy Prentiss

Why visit is important

Making a Complaint

Here are some examples of situations that would lead you to write a letter of complaint:

- You buy something that doesn't live up to its advertising.

- You have a bad experience in a store or other place of business.

- You have a gripe about local, state, or federal services in your community.

- You object to something you see on television.

To get satisfaction in any of these situations, write to the person who is in charge or responsible, and let him or her know how you feel.

Here are some tips to follow when writing a letter of complaint:

- **Be courteous.** Sure, you're unhappy, maybe angry, but you will stand a better chance of getting an answer if you are polite. Remember, the error might have been unintentional. Assume the person to whom you are writing will want to do the right thing.

- **Provide all information.** Give the pertinent details of what happened. If the person has all the facts, they will be better able to respond.

- **Make clear what you expect.** For example, if you received a defective product from the manufacturer, ask to receive a new product. If the solution isn't so obvious, leave it up to the person to whom you're writing to decide what to do.

TIPS

Here are two letters of complaint made by a group of students after a classroom experiment:

48 Duck Lane
Ann Arbor, MI 48105
November 2, 1993

Sugar Nut Company
25 Dodge Street
Hackettstown, NJ 07840

To Whom It May Concern:

Complaint stated

We represent a group of Grade Five students demanding more BeeBees in our 3-ounce king-size package. We found 87 BeeBees in one king-size bag, while we found 112 in another. We have a couple of questions that we hope you can answer:

Specific questions

1. Why are you giving us less BeeBees for our money, while giving other people more? (Is it random packaging?)

2. Do you purposely put in fewer green and orange Beebees than dark brown and yellow? (Or is that random packaging, too?)

3. Would you please consider taking time to look into each package of plain chocolate Beebees so we get an equal amount?

Thank you for your cooperation and time.

Sincerely,

Adam Dinihanian

Mike Mendez

Thomas Henthorn

Dave Mencel

Adam Dinihanian
Mike Mendez
Thomas Henthorn
Dave Mencel

48 Duck Lane
Ann Arbor, MI 48105
November 2, 1993

Sugar Nut Company
25 Dodge Street
Hackettstown, NJ 07480

To Whom It May Concern:

We did an experiment to help us learn about percentages. We used Beebees. We found out what percentage of the bag had red, green, orange, yellow, and light and dark brown. We found out there were the least amount of orange and green.

This experiment caused many questions. How come there are so many yellow, dark brown, and red? Are there so few orange and green ones because of the cost of the food coloring, or is it by accident? Why didn't you have red ones in the Beebees bags for a long time? What is the average number of Beebees in a mini-size bag, regular bag, and king-size bag?

Questions

Now we have some suggestions, too:
1. Try to put more flavor in the candy shells because they'll taste better; and you'll probably get more people to buy them.

Suggestions to improve product

2. Try to put about the same amount of Beebees in each bag. (When we did the experiment with king-size bags, one had 112 Beebees and another bag had 87 Beebees.)

Sincerely,

Sarah Jacobs

Jasmine Hromjak

Sarah Jacobs
Jasmine Hromjak

Offering a Suggestion

Maybe you want to suggest a way to improve a product (or suggest adding a ride to an amusement park, or improving service at your local restaurant).

 Here is a letter that makes a suggestion:

Positive response to product, followed by a suggestion

> 3533 McNair Way
> Lexington, KY 40513
> September 7, 1994
>
> Poppo's Pizza
> 238 Sitwell Place
> San Franciso, CA 94179
>
> To Whom It May Concern:
>
> Your frozen pizza really hits the spot, but there aren't enough pieces. Instead of four pieces in each pizza, why not eight? You could make your pizza a little bigger and make each slice smaller. All the kids would think you are a super nice company.
>
> I hope you will consider my suggestion.
>
> Truly yours,
>
> *Daniel Otfinoski*
>
> Daniel Otfinoski

The company may not act on your suggestion, but you'll probably get a nice reply. You might get something more. As a thank-you, the boy who wrote the letter above got some discount coupons to buy more pizza.

Writing to School and Public Officials

You might write a letter to a person of authority in school or government to make a complaint, suggestion, or request.

Here is a letter to a school principal that contains both a complaint and a request:

864 Hillcrest Drive
Staunton, VA 24401
April 4, 1994

Ms. Sherwood, Principal
Staunton Elementary Schools
719 Woodwell Road
Staunton, VA 24401

Dear Ms. Sherwood:

I am writing to you to discuss how Mrs. Ortega has to walk us up to our lockers after school and then outside to the bus line. I think this is unfair. Other sixth graders leave without their teachers. We are no more noisy or misbehaved than any other sixth graders.

States situation

Complaint and reason

If you would give us just one week to try going to our lockers by ourselves, I'm sure our entire class would appreciate it.

Request

Thank you for reading this letter, and I hope you seriously consider my request.

Thank-you

Sincerely,

Jonathan Warner

Jonathan Warner

Here is a letter of opinion to a public official (in this case the 42nd President of the United States, William J. Clinton, just before his inauguration):

143 Morgan Street
Grover City, CA 93433
January 11, 1993

President William J. Clinton
1600 Pennsylvania Avenue, N.W.
Washington, D.C. 20001

Dear President-elect Clinton:

I am very happy that you will be our President. I'm excited, and I want to hear some of your ideas on making this country better. I would like to suggest three issues that I think you should consider:

Points are specific

1. Economy -- Our economy is falling apart, and we need to improve it in order to make progress.

2. Health care -- America should spend more money on health care so all people can be healthy and enjoy life.

3. Environment -- The natural resources we get from our environment are very special. We need most of them in order to survive. We can't throw them away.

Thank you for your time.

Sincerely,

Toby Anekwe

Toby Anekwe

Letters to the Editor

Most newspapers and magazines have a page or section devoted to letters from readers. These letters are addressed to the editor and are written for a variety of reasons:

- to express an opinion

- to react to another letter, news article, or editorial

- to compliment a person in the community

- to complain about a problem in the community

Whatever kind of letter to the editor you are writing, here are some things to keep in mind as you write:

- **State your opinion clearly.** Be upfront about how you feel. The paper or magazine is giving you an opportunity to say what's on your mind. Don't waste it.

- **Provide reasons for your opinion.** The more convincing your argument, the more people will take your opinion seriously.

- **If you are reacting to another article or letter, identify it.** People won't know what you're reacting to if you don't clearly name it and briefly explain what it says.

- **Be polite.** You can be forceful and direct and still be respectful.

TIPS

Here is a letter to the editor of a local newspaper:

70 Turkey Hill Road
Fort Worth, TX 76156
February 3, 1994

Editor
Fort Worth Star-Telegram
Fort Worth, TX 76156

Dear Editor:

Opinion stated

Reasons for opinion

I believe there should be no homework in the city of Fort Worth. Do we not have school six hours a day, thirty hours a week, one hundred twenty hours a month? I believe we get enough work in school, never mind at home. Our teachers believe we are very hard workers. Imagine, homework on top of sports, on top of after-school activities! We want a break.

Sincerely,

Gregory Trupp
Gregory Trupp

HOMEWORK

Here are two letters to the editor of a news magazine:

24 Hawthorne Drive
Salem, MA 01970
December 10, 1993

Editor
Newsweek Magazine
657 Madison Avenue
New York, NY 10010

Dear Editor:

I don't agree with your November 7 story, "It's the Breakdown of American Families That Is the Primary Cause of Children's Problems." I think the school is at fault, too. If the teachers were more inspiring, the kids would stay off the streets. The schools should at least try to keep them in school.

Name article

Opinion

The family is partly at fault, though. They should set limits for their kids, so they don't hang out with dropouts. If they do, their kids might drop out, too. They might even hang out with gangs that do drugs.

Further explanation of opinion

You can blame both the family and the school. They both need to take care of the child equally.

Sincerely,

Jay Bertini

Jay Bertini

912 Elmwood Drive
New Holland, PA 17557
December 10, 1993

Editor
Newsweek Magazine
675 Madison Avenue
New York, NY 10010

Dear Editor:

Opinion

I recently read William Y.'s November 7th article, "It's the Breakdown of American Families That Is the Primary Cause of Children's Problems." It was true, in my opinion. I agree with most of the article, if not all of it.

Reasons you agree with article

I believe that parents play a big role in society because a parent will steer a child towards success or failure. By supporting a parent in his/her job as parent, and helping him/her, we might have a chance of cracking down on drugs, vandalism, and other crimes teens often get involved in.

This was a great article and I hope to read many more like it.

Sincerely,

John Duggan

John Duggan

Friendly Letters

You might say to yourself, "What's an unfriendly letter?" When we talk about friendly letters, we mean the letters we write to people we like — friends, relatives, or acquaintances.

Whatever the purpose of the friendly letter, all letters of this kind follow the same general format.

Five (Really Six) Parts of a Friendly Letter

Samples of Friendly Letters

Five (Really Six) Parts of a Friendly Letter

▶ Heading

The **heading** gives the month, day, and year, and sometimes the day of the week you wrote the letter. The date is important in case it is delayed in the mail or the person refers to your letter when writing back. If the person you are writing to doesn't know your address, include that above the date.

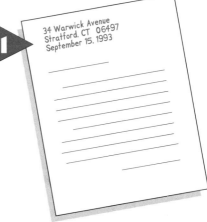

34 Warwick Avenue
Stratford, CT 06497
September 15, 1993

SEE ALSO
Appendix
State
Abbreviations,
p.132

The heading appears in the top right or left corner of the page. Note that the state is not written out, but is abbreviated according to the system used by the U.S. postal service.

▶ Salutation

Salutation is a big word for the greeting of your letter. The most traditional and popular salutation for a friendly letter is **Dear** followed by whatever you call that person (Charlie, Uncle George, Grandma, Dr. Green, etc.) The salutation

N

appears on the left side of the page below the heading. The person's name is followed by a comma.

Dear Lucy,

Dear Uncle Bob,

Dear Dr. Lewis,

Dear Uncle Bob,

What's new with you? Mom says you are coming to visit next month. Could you bring me the photos from your trip to the dude ranch? I want to use them for a report in school. Thanks a lot. Can't wait to see you.

▶ Body

The **body** is the main part of the letter where you write what you have to say to the person. It can be one or several paragraphs, and it should have a beginning, a middle, and an end. Start with a greeting, then tell your news, and end with a good-bye. If your letter deals with more than one subject or topic, you should begin each subject with a new indented paragraph.

Closing

The **closing** is the ending to your letter. Unlike the salutation, there are many closings to choose from. Here are some of the more popular ones: **Sincerely, Your friend, Love, All the best.** Choose the closing that is most appropriate to the person to whom you are writing. For example, if the person is a close friend or a relative, **Love** is a fitting closing. With an acquaintance, you might close with **Sincerely** or **All the best.**

Sincerely,
Your friend,
Love,
All the best,

Signature

The **signature** is especially important because it identifies the letter writer. It should appear directly under the closing. If you are sure the person will know who you are, just sign your first name. If not, add your last name.

A signature is your personal mark, like your fingerprint. It should always be written by hand, even if the rest of the letter is written on a computer or typewriter. Make sure your signature is legible so your correspondent can read it.

6 P.S. (Postscript)

Sometimes when you're finished writing a letter, you remember something else you wanted to say. To avoid having to write the entire letter over again, you can add a postscript. Postscript comes from Latin and means **after writing**. It is a brief addition to the body of your letter, and it appears below the signature. It is always prefaced by the abbreviation **P.S.** Note the word *brief*. If a postscript is too long, you might as well write another letter.

SEE ALSO
Addressing
the Envelope,
p.69

P.S I almost forgot. I'll be back from vacation next Friday. I'll call you then!

Read Your Letter Again!

When you're finished, read your letter over. Take the time to check your spelling, grammar, and punctuation. Make any necessary corrections right on the letter. However, if this gets too messy, copy your letter again. You want the person to whom you're writing to be able to read it.

Here is a friendly letter:
• • • • • • • • • • • • • • • • • •

Heading

34 Warwick Avenue
Stratford, CT 06497
September 15, 1993

Salutation

Dear Uncle Bob,

Body

What's new with you?
Mom says you are coming to
visit next month. Could you
bring me the photos from your
trip to the dude ranch? I want
to use them for a report in
school. Thanks a lot.
Can't wait to see you.

Closing

Love,

Signature

Tom

Postscript

P.S. I almost forgot. I'll be back
from vacation next Friday. I'll
call you then!

Samples of Friendly Letters

A Letter to a Friend

Why write a letter to a friend, especially when you can pick up the phone and call? Here are some reasons:

- You're on vacation.
- You're away at summer camp.
- You have a secret you'd rather write about than say.
- You express yourself better in writing.
- You want to get a letter back.

TIPS

Here are some questions you might ask yourself before writing your letter:

- What did you talk about the last time you spoke (or wrote)?
- What happened that makes you want to write?
- What exciting news do you want to share?
- What's going on with your family?
- What bad news do you want to pass along?
- Is there anything you want to ask?

Here is a letter to a friend who lives in another town:

Date

October 8, 1993

Salutation

Dear Patrick,

Body

How are *you*? Last week we got a new dog. We picked him out at the pound. He's a 9-month-old totally hyper puppy. The vet we took him to said he was part beagle and part English setter. Isn't that weird? I named him Ziggy. When I walk him after school, he sniffs the ground and barks at squirrels, birds, and anything else that moves. He eats everything, and not only dog food. He's already chewed a frisbee, my sister's boots, and two toothbrushes.

Ending

You should get a dog. Maybe when *you* come visit me we'll go to the pound and pick one out. I'm sure your parents would love it if *you* came home with a Great Dane. Yeah, right.

Closing

Your friend,

Signature

Daniel

A Letter to a Pen Pal

A pen pal is someone you get to know through letters. A pen pal is usually someone about your age who lives in another country or region. You get a pen pal's name and address from a club, a kids' newspaper or magazine, or school. When you correspond with a pen pal, you not only make a new friend but learn about a different country or region. Therefore, this letter requires special information. Your letter should include:

- personal details about yourself, your friends and family

- information about your life, the house or apartment you live in, the kinds of foods you eat, how you celebrate holidays

- questions about your pen pal's country and way of life

Don't forget this is a letter and not a questionnaire. Keep your questions brief, and don't lump them all together. Spread them throughout the letter. They should be things you are genuinely curious about.

Here is a pen pal letter:

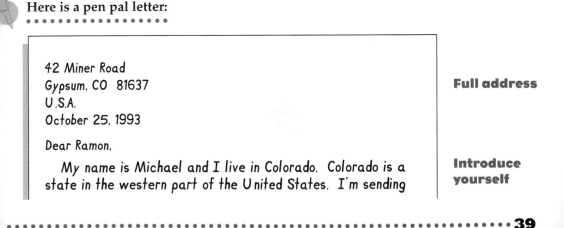

42 Miner Road
Gypsum, CO 81637
U.S.A.
October 25, 1993

Dear Ramon,

My name is Michael and I live in Colorado. Colorado is a state in the western part of the United States. I'm sending

Full address

Introduce yourself

Talk about where you live

What you do every day

Hobbies

Holidays you celebrate

Ending

Postscript

you a map to show you where my town is. There are mountains, canyons, and rivers in Colorado. It's great if you like to hike, fish, or do any other kind of nature stuff.

I live in a small town with my parents and my sister Susan. I'm in the sixth grade. I take history, English, math, and science in school. What subjects do you take in school?

We get a lot of snow in the winter, and I go sledding and skiing. One time our whole school went skiing, even teachers! Does it ever snow in Argentina?

Next week is Halloween. My friends and I dress up in costumes and go trick-or-treating in the neighborhood. This year I'm dressing up as Batman, but with fake vampire fangs (to scare people). Do you dress up for Halloween?

Well, that's all for now. I hope you write soon.

Your Colorado pen pal,

Michael Grose

P.S. I hope you like the stamps on this letter. I picked out ones with dinosaurs because I'm really into them. Do you like to collect stamps? Can you put some good ones on your letter to me?

SEE ALSO Addressing Mail to a Person Outside the United States, p. 73

This letter opens with the writer's entire address, including the country he lives in. It ends with the writer's full name. The pen pal needs that information to write back.

Some pen pals keep in touch for years and exchange stamps, coins, postcards, recipes, books, and other items that tell about their countries and their cultures. Some pen pals even visit each other.

A Letter to a Family Member

You might not think about writing a letter to a family
member you see every day. But you might write to a
favorite uncle or aunt who lives in another state, or to your
dad or mom if one of them is away on a business trip, or to
a sister or brother who is away at school or camp.

Here is a letter to a family member:

March 12, 1993

Dear Dad,

   Hi! How's your trip going? I'm taking care of
things at home. The best part is helping Mom get
Brian to bed at night. It's good to be the boss!
   Guess what? I got an A on my spelling test at
school today! And I only cheated a little (just
kidding). The only word I missed was "dessert." I
know, I know — pretty unbelievable, but true. I
spelled it "desert." What a jerk!
   We all miss you. Especially me. See you soon.
                           Love,

                    Andra

P.S. Mom says hi, too!

A little about home

Something exciting that happened

Ending

A Letter to Someone Who's Just Moved Away

Writing is a good way to keep in touch with friends who have moved away.

TIPS

When writing this kind of letter, keep these tips in mind:

- **Make your letter newsy.** Tell your friends what's going on back home. They will be eager to hear about the latest news in the old neighborhood.

- **Be sensitive.** Your friends may be missing old friends and having a hard time getting used to the new place. So don't go on too much about how great everything is at home. Let them know that they're really missed.

- **Let your friends know you'll keep writing.** Invite your friends to visit you, if possible. You might even suggest visiting each other in the near future.

Here is a letter to someone who's just moved away:

February 11, 1994

Dear Karen,

How are you? Hope you like your new house. What does your room look like?

Bob got a new bike for his birthday last week. His birthday party was fun, but I missed you. He hardly ever lets me use his bike! Big surprise!

The new family that moved into your house seems okay. They have two little boys, and no girls. Just my luck. Maybe I can baby-sit for them.

I have to do my homework now. Write back real soon and send pictures. I promise I'll keep writing.

Do you think maybe you could come back for a visit? Mom said you should come to our house for a long weekend. Wouldn't that be awesome? I miss you.

Still your best friend,

Alice

Questions about the new place

News

Invite your friend to visit

Here is a letter to someone who's moved away written by a younger writer:

269 Park Ave.
Babylon, NY 11702
January 19, 1994

Dear Leanna,

We miss you a lot. We have a new boy. His name is Jonathan. We are doing <u>100 Facts in Mad Minutes.</u> We are learning a lot more in cursive. I found something that had your name on it. We changed tables two times since you left. I wish you could come back!

Love,

Catherine

A Letter to Someone After You've Moved Away

Once you've moved away, your old friends want to know details on your new home, school, etc. And if you want to keep them as friends, let them know you miss them!

Here is Karen's response to Alice's letter. p. 43

February 18, 1994

Dear Alice,

Thanks for your letter! I still feel strange being here. But I'm trying. I'm sorry I missed Bob's birthday party. He is a wild and crazy guy.

Responding to questions

To answer your questions, our new house is way out of town. We have a humongous backyard compared to our old one. I'm sending a picture of me in my room that my mom took.

News

My school is much smaller than ours was. The kids seem nice, but I'm the new kid. You know what I mean?

I'd love to come stay with you! My mom and dad thought I could do it the first weekend in March. How's that for you? Thanks for the invite. I can't wait to see you!

Responding to invitation

Your best friend forever,

Karen

P.S. I'm really glad the people in our old house don't have girls. Ha ha.

Notice that Karen answered all of Alice's questions in her letter and included the picture her friend asked for.

A Letter from Camp or a Trip

When you're away at camp or on vacation, people at home like to know what you're doing.

Here is a letter from someone at camp:

July 20, 1994

Dear Jim,

How's your summer going? Mine's great so far. Camp is cool. There's a lake for swimming and other stuff, lots of hiking trails, and most of my friends are here from last year.

I went canoeing yesterday for the first time. I worked the back paddle, the one that changes directions, so I'm the boat-master. We've got to find a lake when I get back home.

The only things I don't like about camp are the food (I'm living on cereal), morning swim (freeze torture), and my bunkmates snoring at night. But I'm getting used to it all.

I have to end this letter because we're going hiking. I'm going to the top this time! See you in a month.

Your buddy,

Hal

P.S. Write me back. I don't get much mail, except from my parents.

What the camp is like

New experiences

What's coming up

A Letter to Someone Who's Sick

Whether you're sick at home or in a hospital room, a get-well letter is the next best thing to a personal visit. Some people send commercial get-well cards, but a letter is more personal and, therefore, more special. If you do send a greeting card, it's nice to add a personal note.

Here are some tips for writing a get-well letter:

T I P S

⌒ **Be sympathetic.** It's no fun being sick. Let the person know you understand. If it's a serious illness, however, don't write about it. Be positive.

⌒ **Share your experiences.** Maybe you had the same illness as your friend or had to stay in the hospital once. Recall you own experience to show your friend you know what he or she is going through. But don't go on too much about your own problems. You're not the one who needs sympathy.

⌒ **Give some news.** People cooped up in bed are eager to hear what's going on in the outside world. Let them know what's happening at school, in the neighborhood, and with your family.

⌒ **Be cheery.** There is an expression, "Laughter is the best medicine." Cheer up your friend with a joke or a little humor. It'll help him or her forget about being sick.

⌒ **Be accurate.** If your friend is in the hospital, make sure you get the correct hospital name and address. Try to find out and include the hospital room number on the envelope address.

Here is a letter to someone who's sick:

Sharing experiences

A little humor

December 3, 1993

Dear Alex,

I'm sorry you're sick. It's no fun having the mumps. I know. I had them last year. I was in bed for a week! It wasn't so bad though. Mom put a bell by my bed that I could ring every time I needed something. You should get a bell.

Yesterday we had a math test in school. It was tough, but I think I passed it. Aren't you glad you missed it? Having the mumps isn't so bad! Maybe I should catch them again.

Get well soon so we can shoot some hoops!

See ya,

Mark

A Letter to Someone Whose Relative Died

The death of a relative can be one of the saddest times in a person's life. Sympathy cards and letters from friends and relatives are a source of great comfort to the person suffering this loss. Unfortunately, many people feel uncomfortable in this situation and don't know what to say.

As a result, they may put off writing a sympathy letter for weeks. This is a big mistake. People who have suffered such a loss need immediate support from others to help them get over their pain.

Here is some help in writing a sympathy letter:

T I P S

- **Keep it sincere.** A sympathy letter should do just that — express sympathy. It shouldn't exaggerate the sorrow, but address it honestly and simply. You want the person to know you understand their loss and share in it, especially if you knew the relative who has died.

- **Keep it short.** There's no need to go on and on saying how sorry you are. The person is probably sad enough already and doesn't need to read a long, rambling letter. It's enough to know that you care and are there if he or she needs you.

- **Keep it personal.** If you knew the deceased relative, it is appropriate to offer your own memory of him or her, especially something happy or nice. It will make your friend feel better to know that you will also miss this special person.

Here are two letters to people whose relatives have died:

June 27, 1993

Dear Jennifer,

    I am sorry to hear about your grandfather's death. I remember that time he took the two of us fishing. He showed me how to bait the hook and cast. I remember the funny stories he told us, and I'll always remember that day. Your grandfather was a great person, and I will miss him, too.

    Please give my sympathies to your mom and dad, too.

Sincerely,

Jerome

Expressing sympathy

Recalling loved one

March 8, 1993

Dear Dimitrios,

    I was sorry to hear that your mother died. I know she was sick for a very long time. Although I didn't really know her, I'm sure she loved you and your sisters very much and was a great mom. I just want you to know that everyone at school is thinking about you at this sad time.

Your friend,

Angela

What you know

Expressing others' sympathy

A Letter to Someone Whose Pet Died

The death of a favorite pet can be very sad to its owner. Writing to a friend who has lost an animal shows consideration and sympathy.

Here is some help in writing a letter for this situation:

- **Use the pet's name.** Never refer to your friend's dead pet as "your dog" or "your cat." The animal was very special to your friend and should be named.

- **Recall the pet.** Refer to your own experiences with your friend's pet. Mention one of the animal's positive or loveable traits, if possible.

- **Don't talk about getting a new pet.** It takes time to get over a special pet. Do not tell your friend to think about getting another dog or cat or canary. In time he or she may do so, but it's probably not something anyone wants to think about now, when the loss is so painful.

TIPS

Here is a letter in sympathy for the death of a pet:

April 19, 1994

Dear Fred,

I was really sad to hear about Spike's death. I know how much you and your family loved him. Spike was a great dog.

I remember that time we were in the woods, and Spike barked at the big kids that came by. If Spike hadn't been there, they would have messed with us, for sure. Spike was a great protector and a good friend. We'll all miss him.

Sincerely,

Charles

Saying you're sorry

A shared memory

Recalling special traits

A Postcard

Sometimes you want to write someone, but you don't want to write a whole letter. That's when you write a postcard. (It's cheaper to mail, too!)

Here are some tips when writing a postcard:

T I P S

- ✏ **Pick a good one.** The fronts of postcards usually have great pictures. If you're on a trip, you might want to pick one that shows something interesting you've seen.

- ✏ **Give some highlights.** Don't try to tell your friend about everything you've been seeing and doing. You'll never have room for that! Pick out a few highlights to share.

- ✏ **Don't tell any secrets!** Anyone can read what you've written on a postcard, so don't write anything you don't want someone else to know about.

Here is a postcard from a trip. Note where the date and address go.

August 10, 1993

Dear Sam,

   The Grand Canyon's bigger than anything I've ever seen! We must've walked all the way around it. They say there are bears, but I haven't seen any... yet! See you soon!

               Your Friend,

                  Hector

Sam Chee
631 N. Broadway
Hastings-On-Hudson, NY
          10766

Invitations, Thank-you Notes, and Announcements

Invitations

There are basically two kinds of invitations — invitations to a party and invitations to visit.

Inviting People to a Party

Here are some examples of parties that could require a written invitation:

- birthday parties
- graduation parties
- holiday parties
- club or group get-togethers
- housewarmings

Information to Include

You can buy printed invitations at stationery stores, you can make invitations, or you can write a letter. In all cases, make sure to include the following information:

- the type of social occasion

- the date, time, and place of the event (you may want to include written directions or a map)

- information on what to bring or wear

- request for a response to the invitation

Asking for a Response

Asking for a response to the invitation helps you to plan how much food, drinks, party favors, and space you will need. A request for a response is usually written in the lower left corner of the invitation and can take two forms:

R.S.V.P. These initials stand for the French words *repondez s'il vous plait*, which means "please reply." Invited guests should reply by phone (if you include your phone number) or they can send a note to tell if they can come or not.

Regrets Only. These words tell people to respond only if they can't attend. Otherwise, you will assume they are coming.

An invitation should be mailed at least two weeks before the occasion to give people plenty of time to fit it into their schedules.

Here is an invitation to a birthday party:

• •

November 10, 1993

Dear Charles,

I'd like to invite you to my 10th birthday party at my house on Saturday, November 27, at 2 p.m. (Check out the map I included with directions to get here.) We're going to be playing games outside, so don't dress up.

I hope you can make it!

Your friend,

Hank

R.S.V.P. 677-8130

SEE ALSO
Addressing
the Envelope,
p.69

Here is a printed invitation. (We filled it in.)

We're having a birthday party!

Time: Saturday, Nov. 27, 2 p.m.

Place: 10 Langdon Road

For: Hank Evans

R.S.V.P. 677-8130

Accepting an Invitation

If the invitation includes a telephone number, you may accept by phone. If you answer in writing, here are some things to remember:

- **Be prompt**. Don't keep the person waiting to hear from you.

- **Be thankful**. Thank the person for inviting you.

- **Repeat the details**. It doesn't hurt to repeat the time and date to make sure you have them right.

Here is Charles's letter of acceptance to Hank's invitation:

November 14, 1993

Dear Hank,

Thanks for inviting me to your birthday party. I'll definitely be there. See you at your house on November 27 at 2 p.m.

Your buddy,

Charles

Turning Down an Invitation

If you receive an invitation and can't attend, you need to let the person know. This kind of response is called "a letter of regret."

T I P S

Here are some tips for writing this kind of letter:

✐ **Thank the person.** Show your appreciation for being invited, even though you can't be there.

✐ **Give a reason.** Explain briefly why you can't be there. If you don't, the person may think you simply don't want to come.

✐ **Express your regrets.** Let the person know you're sorry you can't come to the party.

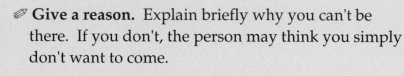

Here is a letter of regret written by another guest Hank invited:

November 15, 1993

Dear Hank,

Thanks for inviting me to your birthday party. Unfortunately, my family is going to my cousin's house in Pennsylvania for Thanksgiving, and we'll be staying there the whole weekend.

It's a bummer that I'll miss your party. But have a happy birthday anyway!

Sincerely,

Larry

Invitation to Visit

There are times when you'll want to invite a friend or relative to your house for the night, a weekend, or school vacation. Here is some information to include when you write this kind of invitation:

- date and length of visit
- things your guest will need to bring
- activities you might do
- request for a response

Here is an invitation to visit:

July 2, 1994
Dear Crystal,

How are you? I miss seeing you at school. How would you like to come visit us the weekend of July 15? You could come on Friday night and stay till Sunday afternoon.

We could ride horses at the stable down the road. And you could take a tennis lesson with me. Let me know if you can come. My dad says we could pick you up at your house.

Your friend,

Rhonda

P.S. My phone number is 347-5029, in case you forgot.

Invitation

Things you'll do

Arrangements

Thank-you Notes

There are two main kinds of thank-you notes — a thank-you note for a gift and a thank-you note for a visit.

A Thank-you Note for a Gift You Like

Thank-you notes let people know that you received their gift and appreciate their thoughtfulness.

Here are some things to keep in mind when writing a thank-you note for a gift:

- **Be prompt.** The note should be written within a week or two of receiving the gift.

- **Be specific.** Maybe it's your birthday and you got many gifts. Mention the gift by name, so the person knows that you know which gift he or she gave you.

- **Explain how you will use/are using the gift.** This shows the gift is something you really need and appreciate.

Here are a couple of thank-you notes for gifts:

Name gifts specifically

> January 7, 1994
>
> Dear Grandma,
>
> I really love the videotapes you sent for Christmas. "E.T." is one of my all-time favorite movies, and I really like "Hook," too. I've already watched them three times each!
>
> Thanks for the movies. Have a happy new year.
>
> Love,
>
> Lauren

SEE ALSO
Addressing
the Envelope,
p.69

July 25, 1994

Dear Mr. Cooper,

How did you know I wanted a basketball for my birthday? I played with it yesterday with some of my friends, and I got four baskets.

Thanks a lot. Now you have to come and see me play basketball this summer.

Sincerely,

Joey Morella

How you will use the gift

A Thank-you Note for a Gift You Don't Like

This is a delicate situation that requires some thought. You don't want to hurt the person's feelings. Here are some pointers:

- **Avoid insincerity.** Don't say you love the gift when you really don't. It's better to say very little than to lie.

- **Focus on the person.** Whether you like the gift or not, it shows the person's thoughtfulness. Thank the giver for thinking of you.

Here are two thank-you notes for gifts you don't like:

•••

August 15, 1993

Dear Uncle George,

Focus on the person

Thank you for the book on trees. It was very nice of you to remember my graduation.

My party was great. Everyone had fun. I'm sorry you couldn't be there. Hope you come visit us this summer.

Take care.

Your niece,

Krio

January 7, 1994

Dear Mrs. Rosenfeld,

Thank you for the pen-and-pencil set for my Bar Mitzvah. I feel like a grown-up person now, except that I still have to go to school.

Jessica's Bat Mitzvah is next month. Get ready for another party!

Yours truly,

Donald Borgen

A Thank-you Note for a Gift of Money

Here are some pointers for writing a thank-you note for a gift of money:

- **Don't mention the amount given.** It's impolite to refer to the exact amount of money. There's also a chance you might mention the wrong amount and confuse the person. Simply refer to it as the "gift of money."

- **Tell what you plan to do with the money.** Let the person know what you're going to spend the money on or what you're saving it for. They'll appreciate knowing it's being put to good use.

Here are two thank-you notes for gifts of money:

March 14, 1993

Dear Granddad,

    Thanks for the money for my birthday. I'm going to use it to save up for a new bicycle. I should be able to buy it real soon. It's red, looks radical, and rides great. Maybe you can come ride with me soon.

                    Love,

                    Arnold

Plan for spending the money

October 12, 1993

Dear Mr. Allen,

  I got the check you sent for my birthday. Thank you for the money. I bought a baseball card album with it. I really needed it because I have about a zillion baseball cards that were all over the place. Now I won't ever lose them. Thanks again.

Sincerely,

Robbie Fisher

How you used the money

A Thank-you Note for a Visit

It is polite to write a thank-you note to friends or relatives after you stayed with them. Here are some things to keep in mind:

- **Don't put it off.** Write your thank-you note within a week after your visit.

- **Mention something that you really enjoyed.** This will make your thank-you note more meaningful and sincere.

- **Extend your own invitation.** Let your friend know he or she is welcome to stay with you, too.

Here is a thank-you note after a visit:

May 9, 1993

Dear Sheila,

Thanks for having me over last weekend. Picking blueberries in the woods behind your house was great! The blueberries tasted better than the ones we buy in the city. And I loved your mom's blueberry pancakes.

Please thank her and your dad. And thank your brother Dave for giving up his bed to me. You have a great family.

Now it's your turn to visit me! You can sleep on the top bunk in my room. (Sally won't mind.) Call soon. How about next weekend?

Your friend,

Tanya

Something you did

Thank household

Invitation

Announcements

Announcements tell people when an event or meeting is taking place. They can be posters or flyers that you hang in noticeable spots (like the bulletin board at school), or you can send the information in a letter. Here are some occasions when you would send an announcement:

- a meeting of an after-school group

- a sports event

- a club party or awards celebration

Information to Include

An announcement should be short and to the point. Here are some of the kinds of information it should contain:

- the group that is meeting

- the purpose of the meeting or event

- the date, time, and place the meeting or event will be held

- the phone number and person to call if someone can't attend

- the admission fee or requirements (dress up, bring food), if applicable

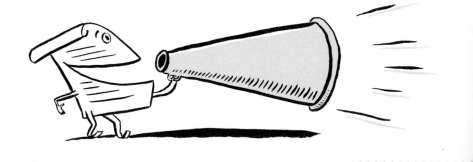

Here is an announcement for a meeting in letter form:

March 22, 1993

Dear Karen,

This is to let you know that the staff of The Addison Advocate, our school paper, will be meeting on Monday, March 29 at 3:30 p.m. after school in the Advocate office. We will be planning our next issue. If you can't make it, please call Frank Bronski at 378-2435.

Hope to see you Monday.

Yours,

Pam Elliot

Editor

Pam gave her full name and title. This kind of announcement is almost like a business letter.

Here is an announcement in a flyer:

Cub Scout Pack 42's Annual Awards Banquet will be held at St. Andrew's Church hall on February 14 at 6 p.m. Scouts will be receiving Tiger Cub, Wolf, and Bear badges, as well as merit and achievement badges. Admission is $3 per family member and will be collected at the door.

Addressing the Envelope

Any letter you want delivered—whether friendly or business—must be sealed in an envelope that is properly addressed.

Three Parts of an Addressed Envelope

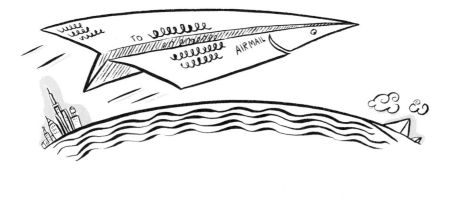

Three Parts of an Addressed Envelope

▶ Return Address

The **return address** is the name and address of the person sending the letter. It is called the "return address" because if the letter can't be delivered, for whatever reason, it will be returned to that address. If you forgot to include the return address, an undelivered letter will end up at a place called "the dead letter office."

The return address usually appears in the top left corner of the envelope and consists of your name, street address, city or town, state, and zip code.

On some personal correspondence, the return address can appear on the sealed flap of the opposite side of the envelope.

```
Juan Rodriguez
13 Spring Road
Little Rock, AR  72205
```

```
        Juan Rodriguez
        13 Spring Road
      Little Rock, AR 72205
```

② ▶ Mailing Address

The **mailing address** is the name and address to which the letter is being sent. It always appears in the center of the envelope.

SEE ALSO
State
Abbreviations,
p.132

In a **personal letter**, the address consists of a name, street address, city or town, state, and zip code. Include an apartment number, if needed.

In a **business letter**, the address on the envelope is the same as the inside address of the letter. There may be separate lines for the title of the addressee (President, Editor, etc.), the division or department the person works in, and the name of his or her company, business, or organization.

Jane Cardwell
President
Quick-Rite Computer Software, Inc.
668 Ripley Boulevard
Los Angeles, CA 21021

If the name of the company or organization is very long, you might want to continue it on a second line, slightly indented.

Quick-Rite Computer
Software, Inc.

Sometimes you will be asked to write a business letter to a department at a business or organization, but you want it to go to a particular person, if possible. Write the word "Attention" followed by a colon and the person's name in the lower left corner of the envelope.

Juan Rodriguez
13 Spring Road
Little Rock, AR 72205

Circulation Department
The Connecticut Post
P.O. Box 1055
Trumbull, CT 06611

Attention: Cal Smith

▶ Postage

A letter will not be delivered without a stamp. The stamp should always be attached in the upper right corner of the envelope. The amount of the stamp depends on the kind of mail you are sending (letter, postcard, package), how fast you want it to get there, and how much it weighs. Ask your family, teacher, or the post office for the correct postage.

Envelope sizes

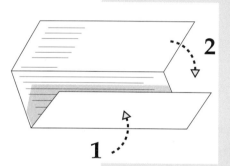

Business letters should be mailed in standard business envelopes, which are rectangular and measure 4 inches by 9 1/2 inches. Personal letters can be sent in any size envelope. The smallest envelope the Postal Service will accept is 3 1/2 inches by 5 inches. A letter, especially a business letter, should be folded neatly in thirds, from the bottom up and the top down, before being sealed in an envelope.

Tips for Addressing an Envelope

- ✐ **Always write the address in ink or on a typewriter.** Never use pencil to write an address. It can be erased or may come off if it gets wet.

- ✐ **Write legibly.** If your handwriting is not completely clear, write the address in block letters or type it. If the mail carrier can't read the address, it will come back to you or end up in the dead-letter office.

Here is an addressed envelope for a business letter:

Martha Jackson
570 Palm Drive
Fort Lauderdale, FL 33329

Editor, Junior Scholastic
Scholastic Inc.
730 Broadway
New York, NY 10003

Addressing Mail to a Person Outside the United States

SEE ALSO
Friendly
Letters
A Letter to a
Pen Pal,
p.39

Any letter being mailed outside the United States requires the name of the country on both the return address and the mailing address. It will require more postage. Remember to write "AIR MAIL" on it to remind the post office.

Here is an envelope addressed to a person outside the United States:

Alex O'Neill
12 Otter Way
Montpelier, VT 05602
USA

Susan Moore
13 Reginald Lane
Milton of Campsie
Glasgow   G65 8EQ
Scotland

AIR MAIL

If you write regularly to a pen pal or friend overseas, you might want to buy some aerogrammes. These light-weight combination stationery/envelopes cost less to mail than regular letters. However, writing space is limited.

Addressing a Package

Address a package the same way you address a letter. Here are some things to keep in mind:

- **Write big.** Packages are usually larger than letter envelopes, and you want to be sure the Postal Service can easily read the address. You might want to write with a marker instead of a ballpoint pen, so the writing will stand out.

- **Include messages for the letter carrier when needed.** If there is something breakable in the package, write FRAGILE on the outside. If the package contains photographs or computer software, write PLEASE DO NOT BEND. Make sure you don't obscure the mailing address with your message.

- **Decide how you want to send the package.** Third class and book rate are cheaper than first class for sending a package, but it will take longer for the package to get there.

Book Reports

Writing a report helps you learn about a topic or book, organize information, and express your thoughts clearly on paper.

Book Reports

. . . .

Tips for Writing Good Book Reports:

- **Give yourself plenty of time.** Don't wait until the last minute to get started. Leave yourself time to think about the book (maybe even talk about it with someone else) before you write your report.

- **Choose a book that you think you'll like.** This may seem obvious, but it is surprising how little time some students spend selecting a book. And if the book you choose bores you, reading and reporting on it will definitely feel like a chore.

> **T I P S**
>
> Here are some tips:
>
> - Skim a few pages to see if you like the writing.
>
> - If you've read and enjoyed a book by an author, look for another book by the same person.
>
> - If you're looking for a nonfiction book, choose one on a topic you'd like to know more about.
>
> - Don't hesitate to ask your teacher or librarian for recommendations.

- **Read the entire book.** Don't just skim the whole book, or your book report will be superficial and weak.

- **Take notes as you read.** Jot down short notes on important things that happen in the story and to the characters. This will keep your thoughts organized and save you time later when you write your report. If there's a particular quote you want to repeat in your report, write down the page number so you can find it later. Remember, don't write or underline in a library book.

- **Summarize.** When writing your book report, don't try to tell everything that happens in the book. Give the highlights of the story. Concentrate on the main characters and what happens to them.

Reporting on a Work of Fiction

Four Parts of a Book Report

If your assignment is to write a short book report on a work of fiction, the teacher just wants to know that you've read the book and understood what it was about. It can be as short as a paragraph or as much as a page. Here are the parts of a short or long book report:

1 Title

The title of a book report is usually the title of the book (underlined or in all capital letters) followed by the author's name. If your teacher has a set format, follow it. And don't forget to include your name!

2 Theme Statement

The theme of the book should be stated in a sentence in the opening paragraph of your book report. The theme is usually the book's main idea.

TIPS

Here are some questions you can ask yourself to figure out the main idea:

- What did the central character in the story learn by the end?
- What was the author's main purpose in writing this book?

> ✐ What feeling or impression did you have when you finished reading the story?
>
> ✐ If someone asked you what this book was about, what would you say?

3▷ Summary of the Story

The **summary of the story** tells about the plot. The plot is what happens to the main characters in the story. Your summary should have a beginning, middle, and end, just as the story does. Make sure you identify each character you name in the summary so your reader won't be confused.

4▷ Your Opinion ⸰

This statement of opinion is often called a **critique**. In a short book report, this should be stated briefly in a sentence or two.

Here is a short book report:
• •

Your name	Brian White
The date	March 15, 1994
Title	<u>Justin and the Best Biscuits in the World</u>
	by
Author	Mildred P. Walter
Theme statement	A good book to read is <u>Justin and the Best Biscuits in the World</u> by Mildred P. Walter. This book is about a ten-year-old boy whose grandfather is a cowboy.
	This book was fun to read because Justin has two sisters who boss him around just like my sisters boss me.

I know how he feels when everybody is on his case and always telling him what to do. Justin's sisters said he could not do anything right. But Justin's grandfather took him to his ranch and showed him how to clean his room, cook, and take care of himself. Now he can do something his sisters can't do. He can make the best biscuits in the world.

I recommend this book to all the people in the world. This book will make you feel good.

Summary

Brief personal opinion

Here is a page-long short book report:

Rebecca Halprin

November 5, 1993

<u>Banner in the Sky</u>
by
James Ramsey Ullman

<u>Banner in the Sky</u> is the story of a young boy who learns that being a man can mean giving up a dream for something more important.

Rudi Matt lives in a small village in the Swiss Alps in 1865. He dreams of climbing the Citadel, a high peak in the Alps. His father died trying to climb the Citadel fifteen years before. Rudi's mother and uncle won't let him try to climb the mountain. But John Winter, an English mountaineer, hires Rudi for his expedition up the Citadel. Rudi's uncle, Franz, also ends up going along as a guide.

Winter is too exhausted to make it all the way to the top, and Franz stays behind to care for him. Another guide, Emil

Setting — place and time

Main characters identified

Longer
summary
of story

Saxo, goes ahead to the top with him.

When the two climbers meet on the mountain, Saxo tries to drive Rudi off and falls to a ledge, injured. Rudi must decide whether to help Saxo back to safety or to continue on to the summit. He brings Saxo down, allowing his uncle and John Winter to reach the summit. They plant Rudi's banner -- his father's red flannel shirt -- on the mountaintop in Rudi's honor.

Personal
opinion

This was an exciting adventure story from beginning to end, and I enjoyed it very much. I would recommend it to anyone who likes a good adventure story.

Long Book Reports

A long book report has the same four parts as a short one but retells the plot in depth, discusses the setting, and analyzes the characters. It also contains a fuller critique, your personal opinion, of the book.

T
I
P
S

Tips for Writing a Critique

Here are some questions to ask yourself as you write your critique:

✐ Did you enjoy the book? Why or why not?

✐ Did the story or characters remind you of your life? Did you identify with any of the characters?

✐ What did you notice about the author's style of writing? Was she or he particularly good at describing things or people? Writing dialogue? Creating suspense?

✐ If there are pictures in the book, how did they add to your enjoyment of the story?

✐ Would you recommend this book to a friend? Why or why not?

Here is a long book report on the same book:
· ·

Nathan Washington

September 30, 1994

<u>Banner in the Sky</u>

by

James Ramsey Ullman

<u>Banner in the Sky</u> is the story of a young boy who learns that there are more ways than one to reach your dream.

Rudi Matt lives in a tiny village in the Swiss Alps in 1865. What he wants most in the world is to climb the Citadel, a high peak in the Alps. Rudi's mother and his uncle, Franz, a mountain guide, want him to give up mountaineering and settle down to working in a hotel. Rudi will not give up his dream, however, and secretly signs on with John Winter, an English mountaineer, who is planning an expedition up the Citadel.

Franz is furious when he finds out what Rudi has done, but he finally agrees to let his nephew go if he goes on the expedition, too. Franz also doesn't want to see Emil Saxo, a guide from another village who Winter has hired, get to the top before him.

Rudi turns out to be a very good climber, but as they get close to the summit, Winter gets sick and can go no further. Franz stays behind, loyal to Winter, but Saxo continues, determined to be the first on the summit. Rudi goes after Saxo, hoping to beat him to the top. When they meet, Saxo fights with Rudi and accidentally falls to a ledge below. Saxo is helpless and injured. Rudi must decide whether to carry Saxo back down to safety or to continue on alone to the summit.

He decides Saxo's life is more important than his dream and helps him down. In the meantime, Winter and Franz have continued the climb, and they reach the summit. Later, when they return to

Longer summary of story

the village, Winter explains that Rudi is the real conqueror of the mountain because of his sacrifice. Through a telescope, Rudi is surprised to see his own banner -- his father's red flannel shirt -- flying on the mountaintop. Winter and Franz had planted it as a symbol of Rudi's triumph.

   I enjoyed Banner in the Sky very much. Ullman, who was a mountain climber himself, writes about the thrill and danger of mountain climbing in a way that makes you feel you were on the expedition. The characters were interesting and acted like real people. Although I really identified with Rudi, I could understand how the other characters acted, even when Emil Saxo tried to hurt Rudi. The suspense of the final climb was totally exciting. I was sorry Rudi didn't get to the top of the mountain, but it was a good ending. I would recommend this book to anyone who likes a good adventure story about people who seem as real as you or me.

Critique and supporting details

Reporting on a Book You Didn't Like

Suppose you start a book for a report, thinking you'll like it. However, by the time you're finished, you find out you didn't like it at all. Now what do you do?

TIPS

Here are some tips to keep in mind when writing a report about a book you didn't like:

✐ **Give your reasons.** It's not enough to simply say you didn't like the book. Give some good reasons for your opinion. Refer to the story, characters, and/or the author's style of writing.

✐ **Find something positive to say.** Few books are all

bad. Try to find something you liked about the book — a character, an event, or some other aspect of the writing — to show you read it carefully enough to have a fair opinion.

✐ **Admit this is only your opinion.** Everyone has different tastes in literature. Try to think of the kind of person who might enjoy this story more than you did.

Here is a critique on the same book, but this writer didn't like it. The critique begins after the summary.

I can't say that I enjoyed this book. It took way too long to get to the final mountain climb. Parts like when Rudi is visited by the spirit of his dead father in the cave were just too weird and didn't fit in with the rest of the book. And the ending was definitely disappointing.

Reasons I didn't like book

Although I didn't like the book, I did enjoy some of the climbing scenes. They were realistic and exciting. I wish the rest of the book had been as exciting. However, if you're really into mountain climbing and don't mind books that take a while to get going, you might enjoy this book more than I did.

One thing I did like

Who might like this book

Reporting on a Work of Nonfiction

Nonfiction includes any story or essay that gives a description of a real event, place, or person.

Five Parts of a Nonfiction Book Report

 Title

 Theme Statement

> In a nonfiction book report, the title and theme statement are the same as in a report on a work of fiction.

Summary of the Book

The summary should cover the main sections of the book. Use the chapters as a guide to discussing the book's events in a logical order. This will also prevent you from getting bogged down in too many details.

Author's Purpose and Point of View

Although the book is factual, it is written from a particular point of view, the author's. In this part of your report, identify what the author's purpose is — to inform, persuade, teach, or entertain.

Your Opinion

In the final paragraph, write if you liked the book or not, and why. Also explain how well you think the author achieved his or her purpose.

Here are some questions you can ask yourself to help you write your critique:

- Did the author provide the information you were expecting to find in this book?
- Was the book written in an interesting and clear style?
- Do you have a better understanding of this subject after reading this book?
- If the author wanted to persuade you, were you convinced by his or her arguments?
- Would you recommend this book to anyone interested in this subject? Even to someone who knows nothing about it?

TIPS

Here is a report on a biography:

Louis Penner

February 20, 1994

And Then What Happened, Paul Revere?

by

Jean Fritz

And Then What Happened, Paul Revere? is a biography of the American patriot and hero Paul Revere. Everybody knows about Paul Revere's midnight ride to warn the country that "The British are coming!" This

Theme statement

entertaining book also talks about many other sides of Paul Revere.

Summary of events in person's life

At age fifteen, Revere took over his father's silversmithing business. He later became a leader in opposing the British and was part of the Boston Tea Party in 1773. After his famous ride, Revere was a money printer, an engraver, a cannon maker, and a soldier. When the war ended and America won its independence, he returned to silversmithing and opened a hardware store. He lived to the ripe old age of 83.

Author's purpose

Mention illustrator

Jean Fritz's purpose in writing this book was to tell people more about an important American, and, at the same time, to tell an entertaining story. What I liked most about this book was the humor, both in the writing and the funny illustrations by Margot Tomes. Any kid who likes American history, especially the American Revolution, will enjoy this book. Kids who think history is boring might change their minds after reading this book.

Research Reports

When you write a research report, you must gather information from several sources and write an account that puts together all the facts and ideas.

Eight Steps to Writing a Research Report

Writing Science Reports

Writing Social Studies Reports

Eight Steps to Writing a Research Report

▶ Choosing a Topic

Most of the time, you will have an opportunity to choose a topic, even if the choice is limited by the assignment. Here are some tips to keep in mind:

- **Choose a topic that interests you.** If you find a topic that excites you, your enthusiasm will show in your report.

- **Choose a topic you can handle.** If a topic is too big, you will not be able to cover it adequately. If it is too narrow, you might not be able to find enough information. For example, if you want to write about dinosaurs, choose one kind of dinosaur or one aspect of many dinosaurs — what they ate or how they protected themselves from enemies.

- **Choose a topic that's off the beaten track.** Avoid the obvious, and your report will stand out from those of other students. For example, if you want to write about an environmental topic, try not to choose a topic that other students might think of, such as recycling. Think about a historic approach, such as how Native Americans related to the environment.

SEE ALSO
Appendix
Sources,
p.141

▷ Researching Your Topic

The library is the logical place to begin research on your topic. See your librarian for help in getting started. You'll probably make use of four main source materials in the library: reference books, periodicals, nonfiction books, and the computer data base.

How To Do Research

Here are some things to remember as you research your topic:

✐ **Use the table of contents and the index.** Focus on the material you need. If a book is all about dogs and your topic is St. Bernards, only read those pages that pertain to St. Bernards. Use the table of contents and the index to find the page numbers for your topic. (Most reference books have an index in the back of the book.) Information on a topic can often be found in a number of places — not just the most obvious ones. An index will cross-reference all the places.

✐ **Write notes on file cards or in a notebook.** Some students prefer to write notes on file cards because they are small and can be arranged and rearranged. Other students like a notebook because it keeps all their notes together in one place. Whichever method you choose, your notes should be concise, clear, and not written in the exact words of the author. By changing the wording you will avoid copying from an author when you begin to write. This is called *plagiarism* (PLAY•jer•izm), and it is a crime. If you want to use a source's exact words, make sure you put quotation marks around them and credit the author.

✐ **Always record sources in your notes (book, author, page number, publisher, date of copyright).** This will help you if your teacher asks where you got a particular fact. You will also need source information when you put together your bibliography, a list of books you used to write your report.

**T
I
P
S**

SEE ALSO
Writing a
Bibliography
p.92

▶ Outlining Your Report

Writing an outline helps you organize your research and plan your report, paragraph by paragraph. However, don't be too attached to your outline once you've started writing. Feel free to change it as you write to keep improving your report.

 Here is an outline for a paragraph of a report:

> The History of Conservation in the U.S.
>
> I. Conservation in Early America
>   A. Native Americans were good conservationists of the land and its creatures.
>   1. didn't wear out one piece of land but moved about from place to place
>   2. only killed animals they needed for food and clothing and shelter
>   3. used every part of the animal, such as buffalo
>   a. ate the meat
>   b. used skin for clothing and shelter
>   c. used bones for utensils and tools

Topic sentence

Supporting examples

Further details

4 ► Choosing a Title

Your title should be brief, descriptive, and say something about the topic that will capture your reader's interest. For example, "Endangered Species in the United States" might be descriptive, but "Danger! U.S. Animals in Trouble" is more descriptive and also will grab the reader's attention.

5 ► Writing a First Draft

The first thing to do is get all your thoughts down on paper, using your notes and outline. Don't worry about punctuation, spelling, and grammar at this time.

Here are some tips to follow as you write:

✐ **Be lively**. Bring your report to life for your reader. Feel free to inject your own personality. Don't just reel off information; make it interesting.

✐ **Be dramatic**. Find a place to dramatize a scene in your report. It might be a scientific breakthrough or a landmark event in a person's life. Use fictional techniques — setting the scene, telling a story, and using actual quotes to bring real characters to life. Avoid using made-up dialogue and events that didn't happen.

✐ **Use interesting details**. Include little-known facts or details about your topic that the reader will find intriguing.

TIPS

6 ► Taking a Break

You've done a lot of work. Now is the time to step back and get a little distance from your report. Put your first draft aside for a day or so. Then you can come back to it, ready to see it from a fresh perspective.

7 ▶ Writing the Final Draft

As you read through your first draft, make any corrections, additions, or deletions necessary.

TIPS

Also ask yourself these questions:

- ✐ Is the title interesting? Does it accurately describe what the report is about?

- ✐ Does the introduction get the reader's attention and present the topic and the main idea clearly?

- ✐ Does the body of the report explain the topic in a logical and interesting way?

- ✐ Are there enough facts and examples supporting the statements made in the report?

- ✐ Does the conclusion sum up what the report is about and bring it to a satisfactory end?

- ✐ Are the grammar, punctuation, and spelling correct throughout?

Make a final check!

- **Include your name**
- **Look for misspellings**
- **See if pages are numbered**

After you revise your draft, share it with a friend or family member. Someone may see a way to improve your report that you didn't think of. A fresh set of eyes can pick up mistakes that you may have missed. Now write your final draft.

8 ▶ Writing a Bibliography

A bibliography is a list of books, articles, and other sources you used in your research. It is alphabetized according to the authors' last names. It shows the reader where you got your information and suggests other sources the reader can use to find out more about your topic.

Here is a book entry in a bibliography:

author

title of book

Whitney, David C. The American Presidents. New York:

Prentice Hall Press, 1990.

city of publisher

publisher

year of publication

Here is a periodical entry in a bibliography:

author

title of article

Ebert, Alan. "Oprah Winfrey Talks Openly About Oprah." Good Housekeeping, September 1991.

publication in which article appeared

date of publication

A CD-ROM disk might be listed like this:

title of the disk

The Presidents: It All Started With George Washington.

Washington, National Geographic Society, 1992

city of publication

publisher

year of issue

If you interview someone, list that person in a separate section.

SEE ALSO
Appendix
Sources,
p. 142

when interviewed

Ford, Alan. Interview, October 15, 1993.

person interviewed

Writing Science Reports

A science research report can be one of three kinds:

- an account of an experiment

- an exploration of a topic of scientific interest

- the story of a scientist's life and work

Reporting on an Experiment

A report on an experiment has three basic parts: the hypothesis, the experiment, and the conclusion.

1▶ Hypothesis

A **hypothesis** is a statement that can be tested by an experiment to see if it is true. You should state your hypothesis simply and directly in a sentence. It should be preceded by the word Hypothesis and a colon. For example:

Hypothesis: Mold grows more easily under warm, moist conditions than under cool, dry conditions.

2▶ Experiment

The experiment part consists of three sections:

- the list of materials you used

- the numbered steps you performed

- the results

3▶ Conclusion

In the conclusion, you tell what the experiment shows and how it proves or disproves your original hypothesis.

Each action you perform is a separate step. Write each step clearly and simply. Take notes during the experiment so you don't forget anything.

Here is a report on an experiment on salt and ice:

An Experiment on Salt and Ice

by

Roger Nelson

HYPOTHESIS: Salt lowers the melting point of water and can be used effectively to melt ice.

Hypothesis

EXPERIMENT

MATERIALS: a glass of water, a piece of string several inches long, an ice cube, a filled salt shaker

List of materials

PROCEDURE:

1. I placed the ice cube on the surface of the water-filled glass.

Steps listed clearly

2. Next I tied a 1" loop in the piece of string and held the string over the ice cube so the loop end touched the top of it.

3. Then I shook some salt on top of the ice cube where

Results

the loop of string sat. I waited for a few minutes.

    4. I picked up the string. The loop stuck to the cube, and I could lift it right out of the water glass.

Relates results to hypothesis

CONCLUSION: The salt caused the ice to melt around the string. Then the water froze again and froze the string to the ice cube. This is why I was able to lift up the string with the ice cube attached. The results of the experiment prove my hypothesis that salt is an effective ice melter.

Reporting on a Research Topic

This kind of report can be on any science topic.

- weather conditions
- geological features
- animals
- plants and trees

- space exploration
- electricity
- the environment
- computer technology

Here are some tips for writing a research report on a science topic:

T I P S

✐ **Narrow your topic.** This can't be emphasized enough. Many students take on a topic that is too general or too large to cover comfortably in one report. Animals is obviously too broad a topic, but so might be animals of Australia. A more focused topic would be one particular Australian animal, such as the koala bear, the kangaroo, or the platypus.

✐ **Use periodicals in your research.** Scientific knowledge is always expanding. Consult newspapers, recent scientific magazines, such as *Popular Science* and *Natural History*, and those written for young readers, such as *Science News* and *Science World*.

✐ **Include a visual aid in your report**. A chart, diagram, or photograph can give your reader a better understanding of the topic. For example, if you were doing a report on a plant or animal, you might include a diagram naming all its parts.

SEE ALSO
Appendix
Sources,
p.141

Three Parts of a Report on a Topic

▶ **Introduction**

The introduction presents your main idea about the topic and sets the tone for the entire report. It should capture your reader's interest immediately.

Here is an introduction to a report on a research topic, the platypus:

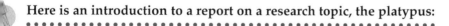

<pre>
            The Incredible Platypus
                     by
              Martin Slotkin

    Near the end of the 18th century, the skin of a
strange animal arrived from Australia at a
laboratory in London, England. The animal had the
bill and webbed feet of a duck and the skin of a
beaver. Some scientists who saw the skin called it
a hoax. But one man, Dr. Irving Shaw, believed it
was real. He named the animal platypus, which is
Greek for "flat-footed." Nearly two hundred years
later, the platypus is still one of the strangest
animals on earth.
</pre>

Dramatic opening

Suspense

Main idea

Body

The body of the report contains information and details that tell about the topic and support the main idea.

- It should have a topic sentence that the other sentences relate to or support.

- Each paragraph should follow the next in a logical, organized sequence.

- The body of a research topic report discusses different aspects of the topic.

- The body of a report on a person follows the person's life, focusing on his or her scientific achievements. Enrich the body with quotes and visual aids.

Here is the body of the report on the platypus:
• •

**Topic
sentence**

**Term
defined**

**Supporting
details**

```
   The platypus may look like a helpless animal, but
it isn't. All male platypuses have a hollowed, claw-
like projection called a "spur" on their hind legs. It
is connected to glands that secrete poison.
Scientists believe the platypus uses the spur for
defense.  The poison is not deadly, but drugs a
victim when it is ejected through the spur into the
prey's skin. One man hit in the hand by a platypus's
spur couldn't move his hand for nine weeks!
```

3 ▶ ## Conclusion

The conclusion brings the report to a satisfactory end by summarizing the main idea in a few well-chosen sentences.

Here is the conclusion of the report on the platypus:
• •

> The platypus is truly an amazing creature. With all its oddities, this animal is well adapted to its environment. Although it is believed by scientists to be among the most primitive of mammals, the platypus is an animal whose mysteries are only beginning to be understood.

Repetition of main idea

Satisfying closing

Here is a short science report on a seahorse by a young writer:
• •

About the Seahorse.
by
Amanda Altman

A seahorse is a very weird kind of fish. It moves only a few times a minute. It swims by grabbing on to plants and moving the fin on its back. One amazing thing is that the seahorse moves its back fin 60 times per second. They have two skeletons which most fish don't have. Seahorses eat little green shrimp. The biggest a seahorse can grow is two feet.

Title states the topic

Main idea

Supporting facts

Reporting on a Person

SEE ALSO
Social Studies
Reports
Reporting on
a Person,
p.103

A report on a scientist should give the reader an understanding of events in the person's life that influenced her or his career in science. It should explain some of the work the scientist has done. The parts of this report are the same as for a report on a topic: Introduction, Body, Conclusion. Look for information on Writing a Report on a person in the next section on Social Studies Reports.

Writing Social Studies Reports

Three kinds of social studies reports are:

- on a place
- on a social issue
- on a person

Reporting on a Place

SEE ALSO
Business
Letters
Asking for
Information,
p.16

You might want to write a report on a place you would like to visit someday, such as the pyramids of Egypt or the outback of Australia. Or, you might want to report on someplace close to home, such as the state capital or a Revolutionary War battlefield.

T
I
P
S

Either way, here are some questions to answer as you plan your report on a place:

✍ Where is this place?

✍ What are the geographic features and climate of this place? How do these affect the people and wildlife that live in or near it?

✍ What other places border on this place? How does location influence the place and its neighbors?

> ✐ What kind of people, if any, live in this place? How do they live? What do they do for a living? What are their homes like?
>
> ✐ What is the historical background of this place? How does its past affect its present?
>
> ✐ Have you visited this place? If so, what are your personal impressions?

Possible Subtopics for a Report on a Country or State

If the place you choose for a topic is a country or state, here are some subtopics you may want to include in your report:

- location
- cities
- people
- natural resources
- form of government
- settlement and history
- industry and agriculture
- religion
- food
- climate

If you discover there is too much material for one report, narrow your topic to one aspect of a country or a state, such as the natural resources of Spain or the Native American culture of New Mexico.

Reporting on a Social Issue

Newspapers, magazines, and television news will provide you with many ideas for this kind of report.

Here are a few:

- gun control
- health care
- population control
- education
- the environment

- censorship
- children's rights
- consumer protection
- influence of media
- the homeless

TIPS

Here are some useful tips to keep in mind when writing a report on a social issue:

✎ **Show all sides.** If the issue you are reporting about is a controversial one, present all sides of the issue. This way readers can make up their own minds. You may present your own point of view in the conclusion.

✎ **Use up-to-date sources of information.** Don't confine your research to books and encyclopedias. Use magazines, newspapers, radio, and television to make sure your research is up-to-date and relevant.

✎ **Include statistics and visual aids in your report**. Visual aids that clearly illustrate your points can make your report more effective. Good visual aids for a social studies report include maps, charts, and time lines.

SEE ALSO
Appendix
Using
Common
Reference
Tools,
p.137

Reporting on a Person

A social studies report can be about a person who is famous, or an ordinary person whose experiences were important in history or the news.

Here are some of the different kinds of people you might consider:

- soldiers
- business leaders
- explorers
- political figures
- athletes
- journalists

- writers and artists
- community leaders
- thinkers and educators
- religious leaders
- entertainers
- activists in social movements

Here are some tips to keep in mind when writing a report on a person:

T I P S

⬦ **Choose someone you admire.** If you like the person you've chosen, you're more likely to write a report that is interesting and informative.

⬦ **Use primary sources whenever possible.** A primary source is something spoken or written by the person or someone who knew her or him personally. Good primary sources include autobiographies, letters, quotes in contemporary newspaper and magazine articles, and personal interviews. When quoting from a primary source, make sure you give the source credit in your text and in your bibliography (include the author, work, and page number). Also be sure to put quotation marks around the person's exact words.

SEE ALSO
Writing A Bibliography, p.92

Appendix Sources People, p.142

- Highlight any events in the person's life that helped ensure his or her success.

- Discuss setbacks that may have taught the person an important lesson.

- Stress the person's achievements. Focus on what this person did that is worth the reader's attention.

Three Parts of Any Social Studies Report

1▶ Introduction

The introduction to a social studies report presents the topic, whether it be a place, issue, or person. Present your topic in a way that makes your reader want to know more about it. This may be done with a dramatic scene, a descriptive picture, or a startling statistic. Your introduction should also contain the main idea about the topic that you will further explain and explore in the rest of the report.

 Here is an introduction for a report on a place:

<u>Inside the Sahara</u>
by
Amy Dubcek

Descriptive word picture

It is three and a half million square miles of sand, rocks, plateaus, and mountains about the size of the United States. It covers parts of ten countries, but its main inhabitants are snakes, lizards, and gerbils. Much of it gets less than one inch of rain a year. The highest temperature on record, 136°F, was recorded there. Its name means "desert" in Arabic. It is the Sahara, the world's largest desert.

Amazing statistic

Suspense-building lead-in

Here is an introduction for a report on an issue:

• •

Elisabeth Kiernan
Grade 4
Babylon Grade School

Pulling Together in the Face of Disaster

On August 24, 1992, Hurricane Andrew struck Homestead, Florida. Homestead, Florida was destroyed. The land and homes were ruined. The wind speeds from this storm were up to one hundred and four miles per hour.

Strong dramatic opener

After the storm, the results were devastating. Eighty-five thousand homes were destroyed. One hundred eighty thousand residents were left homeless. Hurricane Andrew left twenty billion dollars in damages and repairs.

Startling statistics

Here is an introduction for a report on a person:

<u>Benjamin Banneker</u>

by

Kelly Thompson

Dramatic opener

President George Washington was worried. The fate of the future capital of the United States was in jeopardy. The architect of the new city of Washington, Major Pierre Charles L'Enfant, had just quit the project and taken all his plans with him. It would take years to build the city without those plans.

As the President expressed his fears to the team that had been working with L'Enfant, an assistant surveyor quietly said he knew all of L'Enfant's plans by memory and could reproduce them. The President was amazed, but the surveyor soon proved what he said was true.

Effective summary of achievements

African American Benjamin Banneker -- astronomer, almanac summary writer, mathematician, and surveyor -- was about to add another triumph to his list of achievements: U.S. capital builder.

2 ▶ **Body**

The body of the report expands and explores the topic.

- In a report about a place, the body describes features of the place. These may be in separate paragraphs or even separated by subtopic headings.

- In a report about an issue, the issue may be examined from both pro and con positions.

- In a report on a person, the person's life and achievements are explored in chronological order.

Here is a paragraph from the body of the report on the Sahara (cont'd from p.105):

> ### The Sahara's People
>
> About two million people make their home in the Sahara. Most of them are <u>nomads</u>, wandering groups of people who drive their herds of sheep, goats, or camels in search of grass and water. Most of these nomads are Arabs or <u>Berbers</u>, a non-Arab people who live in northern Africa. There are also people who live in small communities built around natural or human-made watering holes, called <u>oases</u>. They work on small farms and grow barley, wheat, and dates.

Important terms defined

Here is a part of the body of the report on Hurricane Andrew (cont'd from p.105) :

Topic sentence of paragraph

Some people coped well, and others didn't. Some people started looting because there wasn't electricity, and at night when everything was dark, people could not watch over their homes or stores unless they stayed up all night. Looters carried guns and took whatever they could. Fighting and violence took place.

The Red Cross and the National Guard soon came through. They brought shelters, clothing, food, and water to Florida. So many people were homeless and starving that tent cities were set up. Tent cities gave the people homes. Food was given out buffet style.

Here is a paragraph from the body of the report on Benjamin Banneker (cont'd from p.106):

Important episode from youth

When Benjamin Banneker was young, you could already tell that he would be someone special. Once, an old man gave Benjamin a pocket watch as a present. Benjamin took it apart to see how it worked and put it back together. A local schoolteacher who lived near Benjamin's farm in Maryland gave him a journal with a diagram of a clock. Benjamin used the diagram and his pocket watch as models for building his own clock. He made the whole thing out of wood. It took him two years to finish. It was the first clock built in the U.S., and people came from all over the Middle Colonies to see it. It kept nearly perfect time for over fifty years.

3 ▶ Conclusion

In a social studies report on a place or a person, the conclusion repeats the main idea and sums up what you have to say about your topic. In a report on an issue, the conclusion can sum up the different sides, present your personal feelings and thoughts, and offer possible solutions.

Here is a conclusion for the report on the Sahara Desert (cont'd from p.107):

> Over centuries the Sahara has gotten drier and larger. Some experts feel the Sahara is still expanding because there are droughts on the Southern border. Other people claim the droughts are part of the natural cycle of the desert. Either way, the Sahara is one of the world's toughest and most amazing environments.

Possible future developments

Restatement of main idea

Here is a conclusion for the report on Hurricane Andrew (cont'd from p.108):

> Even today the people in Florida still haven't recovered, but everyone can learn from this disaster. Instead of violence, people should always try to work things out peacefully. I really learned from this lesson. I hope you have, too!

Here is a conclusion for the report on Benjamin Banneker (cont'd from p.108):

● ● ● ● ● ● ● ● ● ● ● ● ● ● ●

Final summary of achievements

Topic sentence of report reworded

Benjamin Banneker died in 1806, but his legacy lives on today. He was the most famous African American of his day and for good reason. He built the first clock in the United States. He helped build our permanent capital city. He predicted an eclipse of the sun. He wrote one of the most popular almanacs in the United States. He spoke out against slavery in letters to the United States' third president, Thomas Jefferson. Benjamin Banneker was truly a great American.

Here is a complete report on a person with an unusual approach. The writer chose to write as if Annie Sullivan were telling her own story.

● ● ● ● ● ● ● ●

Annie Sullivan
by Alex Brucculari

I'm Annie Sullivan. When I was a child my eyes weren't too good, and when I started to rub them they got red. I lived in a poor family. I was born April 14, 1866. I was baptized by the name of Joanna, but everyone called me Annie.

I was brought to a poorhouse when I was ten because my parents had died. I had a brother named Jimmie. He was younger than I and had a lump on his hip. That's how our mother died. I was very small for my age and didn't know how old I was, so the people at the poorhouse guessed my age. They thought I was eight, but I was really ten.

One time in the middle of the night, I woke up and found my brother dead. I screamed and cried and woke the whole poorhouse. Lights came on, and people ran to help me. I didn't know they were there to help me. I thought they were going to take me away. I started to bite and cried harder. For the next couple of days I had to cry myself to sleep.

When I was old enough to get a job I was blind. I got some operations. The second operation worked. My vision was blurry, but at least I could see. Later I got glasses and could see very well.

I went to school, and when I graduated I got another job. It was teaching a deaf, blind and mute little girl, Helen Keller. Helen's mother and father felt bad for her and let her eat off of other people's plates. I had to teach her not to and even had to grab her. It took a long time before I could actually teach Helen things.

Finally, we were out pumping water when I thought about it. I took Helen's hand and put it under the water so she could feel it and know what it was by feeling it. It took lots of patience. Finally, we started to talk with our hands. I graduated with Helen and managed to help her finish her last book. Then on October 19, 1936, I died.

Here is a complete report on the Shoshoni:

How the Shoshoni Got Their Food

by Ben Pred

Shoshoni lived in the mountains where there was not much food. In the mountains they ate squirrels, grasshoppers, sheep, antelope, and birds. Once a year or so, the Shoshoni would go to the plains for a buffalo hunt. Some would go to the woods for seeds, berries, and small birds. Another group would go swimming for salmon.

Some Shoshoni used branches or animal hides to build their homes. Some Shoshoni dug shelters in the hillside. They played a kind of football with a ball made of animal skin stuffed with rabbit hair. But they didn't have much time to play. They had to build their homes and find food. In many ways, the Shoshoni had it much harder than the Iroquois. The Iroquois had salmon, deer, and other fish and animals. The Shoshoni only went hunting once a year, and they ate grasshoppers. I think I would have liked to be an Iroquois.

Essays And Reviews

Essays

Reviewing Movies and Television Shows

Essays
• • • • • • • •

An essay is a short composition that has one main idea. An essay may require research, and it often contains the writer's opinions, as well.

Three Kinds of Essays

Explanatory Essays

An explanatory essay tells about something or explains how to do something. Its purpose is to inform. It should be written in a straightforward, clear style. For example, you could write an essay called "Making Steam from Trash" in which you explained the technology used in burning garbage to make steam to create electricity.

Persuasive Essays

In a persuasive essay, the writer tries to persuade the reader to accept an idea or agree with an opinion. The writer's purpose is to convince the reader that her or his point of view is a reasonable one. The persuasive essay should be written in a style that grabs and holds the reader's attention, and the writer's opinion should be backed up by strong supporting details. You might write a persuasive essay on "Why Our School Library Should Remain Open After School."

Humorous Essays

A humorous essay takes a light-hearted look at its subject. This doesn't mean it is filled with jokes. It means that its main purpose is to entertain. In a humorous essay you might offer your zany idea on "How the Gladiator Became the Symbol of Laurel Middle School."

Steps to Follow When Writing Essays

- **Choose a topic carefully**. Pick a topic that interests you and that you know something about. Ideally, it is a subject or issue on which you have strong opinions.

- **Define your main idea**. Your main idea will help you focus your thoughts and research your topic. It is partly determined by your purpose — to inform, persuade, or entertain.

- **Organize the body of your essay carefully**. After gathering your research and ideas, make an outline. If your purpose is to persuade, place your most persuasive argument first and follow it with the other arguments in order of importance. If your purpose is to inform, give each feature of your subject a paragraph to itself. If your purpose is to inform by instructing, order each step in sequence. Even a humorous essay should be organized so that the reader is swept into your point of view.

SEE ALSO
Writing Social Studies
Reports
Reporting on a Social Issue, p.101

Four Parts of an Essay

All essays have four parts.

1 Title

The title should be descriptive and set the tone for the entire essay.

2 Introduction

The introduction is the first paragraph of an essay. Its purpose is to
- let the reader know the essay's purpose: to explain, persuade, or entertain
- introduce the author's opinion and/or purpose
- grab the reader's attention

3 ► Body

The body explains or supports the main idea. It is usually several paragraphs long.

4 ► Conclusion

The conclusion repeats the main idea in a new way and brings the essay to a satisfying end.

Samples of Essays

Here is an explanatory essay:

Descriptive title

Important opening statistic

Important information

Steps to take

Conclusion

<u>Animal Testing</u>

By Jessica Parker

Did you know that over five million animals are killed each year in laboratories for testing? Whenever you buy a product that has been tested on animals, you are supporting the killing of the kinds of animals that you might have for a pet.

Rats, rabbits, mice, cats, dogs, birds, gerbils and hamsters are being tested at this very moment. Over five hundred mice a day are being injected with window cleaner by a well-known manufacturer, for example. Rabbits are getting hot, melted lipstick forced into their eyes. If you wouldn't be willing to be treated like this, why should these animals be willing?

Here are some ways that you can prevent this cruelty:

1. Ask companies that test on animals to use a computer-like machine that is almost as accurate as an animal. They can use it over and over again.

2. Look at the labels of cosmetic products to see if they are tested on animals.

3. Ask the sales person if the product is tested on animals.

4. Write letters to environmental groups, and ask about animal testing.

5. Join protests and rallies against animal testing.

6. Tell your friends what you have learned from these suggestions, or how they can help.

If enough people protest this cruelty to animals, maybe we can stop it.

Here is an explanatory essay by a younger writer:

Spoolmobile
by
Erica Sterling

When our class made spoolmobiles, we had a lot of fun doing it. It was really easy. First you take a rubber band and put it around a straw. Then you take a washer and put it through the rubber band. Next take the rubber band and stick it through the spool. Then you take a stirrer and cut it and stick it through the rubber band. Last, take a piece of tape and put it on the stirrer. When you finish it, put it on the ground and turn the straw and let go of it, and it should roll. The more you spin it, the more it will roll. I really enjoyed doing it. It is a fun project.

Here is a persuasive essay:

Nonviolence: Making It Work Today
Example: Environmental Violence
by
Tim Ruggeri

There are many problems in the world today that can't be helped, but some problems can be solved. Environmental violence is one that can. People dumping waste and killing animals can be stopped, but only with a lot of people's help. I am writing this essay so I can tell you about some of these issues, like killing animals, or offshore dumping, and how they can be stopped. I think this goes with Martin Luther King's second principle: The beloved community is a world of peace with justice.

Main idea sentence

Naming an authority

Argument

People killing endangered animals are doing something that is hurting others. Pretty soon they might find themselves killing the last of that species. All kinds of animals, even our nation's bird, the bald eagle, are becoming extinct and they must be helped.

Another important environmental violence issue is that some people don't know what to do with toxic waste so they just dump it in the ocean, not thinking about what they have just done. They have just contaminated our ocean and probably killed a lot of animals that live in the water. People also dump garbage in the water that some animals will think is food, and when they eat it they will die because they will choke.

Conclusion

Martin Luther King believed that communities should work together to make peace, and people dumping waste and killing animals aren't doing what he is saying. This affects me because the pollution will be there for years to come unless someone stops this. There are not many ways to stop this, but there are a couple of possible solutions. One of them is to write letters to Congress to try to pass a new law to fine anybody who is caught doing any of these bad deeds. Another is to donate some money to a wildlife refuge.

Here are two humorous essays:
• •

Creative title

Tales From the Chair

by R. Katie Barnes

Clever introduction

Junior High means more than just lockers and desks; for us unfortunate many with un-perfect teeth, it also means braces. I've had my braces since I was four and am getting ready to celebrate a decade of dental wear! Yay! It's not just the gumlessness, aching, or wire, not even the ability to pick up radio signals in my mouth that makes braces so annoying. It's the dreaded CHECK-UP!

It's pretty routine. My mom takes me out of my

favorite class (lunch) so that I can go to the dentist's office.
Once I'm there, I sit for an hour in an uncomfortable chair,
staring at the latest issue of <u>Bug Collector's Monthly</u>,
until a perky woman in a blue suit and plastered smile
calls me into the dentist's room. Before I know it, another
woman has come in and whisked a bib around my neck
and has a 1,000,000 watt bulb shining in my eyes. Then
she inserts a device into my mouth which greatly stretches
apart my lips and surrounding facial structures, until they
are pressed firmly against my ears. She then asks me my
name, what grade I'm in, what school I go to, how old I
am, and anything else she can think of, as if I can answer
with half of my face immobilized. Then, she whips out a
miniature monkey wrench and directs it towards my now
over-stretched mouth. After several futile attempts, she
manages to pull out the wrong thing.

"Oops," she giggles. "Better get that blood."

Before I have time to make a break for it, the head
dentist enters. I am content to let him examine my
battered mouth, because a visit by the head dentist
usually means the end is near. He then leaves me in the
incompetent hands of the dreaded cheerful assistant. She
tries to make pleasant conversation as she destroys what
few teeth I have left. She babbles on and on, and I try to
tune her out. She apparently thinks of me as teeth with
ears.

Several hours and about 300 mistakes later, she's done.
I am whisked to the waiting room where my mom seems
grateful to see me. Perhaps she heard my muffled
screams of anguish. I look at her watch to see how many
days I've been there. 12:30! That can't be! I haven't even
missed Algebra!

As I approach the door that leads to sunshine and
freedom, the office assistant hands me a balloon. "Please
come again," she pipes in her sickeningly sweet voice.
The balloon has a large smiley face on it, and I decide to
keep it in my room, as a reminder to what lies in the
future — my fateful trip back to THE CHAIR....

Main idea

Increasing exaggeration

Ridiculous conclusion

Jennifer Brehm   March 12, 1994
Writing   Ms. Mastrandrea

The Human Clock

Hi! I am a time. I know because everyone always points to me and says, "Look at the time!" They say time flies when you're having fun, but I most certainly do not fly. I sit pinned to the wall. I hate it when people turn my wheel because my hands turn all over my face and it twists my nose around. So I get back at them! I make good times go fast and bad times go slow. On a special night, all times go back an hour. This makes people get mixed up with the time.

I work in a very unique way, as I have three hands. My second hand is always in a hurry to get somewhere, and my hour hand thinks he has all the time in the world. I like my minute hand. She's just right.

Once I saw a poor little time strapped to a person. He looked sad because he was strapped onto this person so he couldn't move. I then told him about my grandfather who is so bossy and has such a loud voice. Next I told him about the times who are chained to people, so he would know he wasn't the only one that was sad. There are others with the same feelings just like himself. Finally, I told him how I felt when the kids at school scream and run away at the end of the day, leaving me alone. This makes me feel like I am a monster. This is my life as a clock. Sometimes it's interesting, sometimes it's not.

Answering Essay Test Questions

Essay test questions are in-depth questions that cannot be answered in a few words, but require at least a paragraph. Like an essay, an essay question has a main idea that you must recognize to answer the question fully and satisfactorily.

Here are some useful tips for writing answers to essay test questions:

- **Read directions and questions carefully**. To answer a question concisely, look for clue words that indicate how a question should be answered. These words include explain, compare, illustrate, summarize, and contrast.

- **Restate the question as a declarative sentence**. If the question says, "Why did the American colonists oppose the Stamp Act? Give at least two reasons," your answer might begin, "The two most important reasons that American colonists opposed the Stamp Act were..."

- **Be concise and focused**. Avoid including unnecessary information. Don't repeat yourself. Answer the question as thoroughly as you can and then move on to the next one.

- **Use scratch paper, if allowed, for writing down ideas**. This will enable you to jot down thoughts or outline your answers without messing up your test page.

- **Leave time to go over your finished work**. Allow yourself time to go back and make — as neatly as possible — any necessary corrections in punctuation, grammar, or spelling.

T I P S

Here are three essay test questions and their answers:

Clue word

Describe how you might feel if you were rescued from slavery by Harriet Tubman. What are you thinking? What are you doing? Where are you?

Descriptive scene

I was just getting to sleep when someone knocked on the door. My mom went to get it. "It's Moses!" she cried. "You've come to get us!"

"Shh!" the person at the door said. "Now get your things. We're going on a long trip."

Who, what and where

I packed up some of my stuff, and we set out to the North. At first I thought we had been sold, but when I saw the lady's face I knew we were fine. It was Harriet Tubman. As we were walking, I heard hooves. We were being chased. I hurried up a little. At about 5:00 a.m. we laid down on the moss and went to sleep. We could only travel at night.

Supporting details

When I woke up it was midnight. We still had a few hundred miles to go. We had a breakfast of nuts and berries. We finally got to a station where the people gave us food and directions. We were still miles away from Canada.

On Friday we made it. We crossed the Mason-Dixon line, and we were free. I was so happy, I hugged Harriet. It felt so good to be free!

<u>Describe</u> the main characteristics of mammals.

Clue word

There are four main characteristics of mammals that make them different from all other animals. Mammals nurse their young and take care of them longer than other animals. Mother's milk is the first food for human babies, as well as dogs and cats. Opossums and kangaroos are so protective of their young that they carry them around in a pouch. Mammals are the only animals that have hair on their bodies. Some are covered with thick hair, like bears, while others only have hair at certain times of life. Some whales only have hair before they are born. Mammals have bigger and more highly developed brains than other creatures. Among the most intelligent are humans, pigs, dolphins, and apes. Finally, all mammals are warm-blooded. This means their body temperature stays about the same even if the temperature around them changes.

Using wording of the question

Good examples

Interesting fact

Defining term to show understanding

Clue word

Explain what it would be like to live in King Arthur's time.

Use wording of question

In King Arthur's time you couldn't just go to the fridge or the bathroom for water. You had to go to a stream or a well. And you couldn't watch cable T.V.! Boy, what torture! The only book to read was the Bible. They didn't have printers back then, either. A nun or a monk might spend forty years copying the Bible.

Interesting fact

Back then, some people were accused of being witches. If you were accused, the people would give you the water test. They would throw you in the water. If you drowned, you were innocent. If you stayed afloat, you were burned at the stake. Only a witch could float!

Reviewing Movies and Television Shows

A review of a movie or TV show is similar to a review of a book. Whether it is as short as one paragraph or as long as a few pages, there are four parts.

Four Parts of a Review

1▶ Title

The title is usually the title of the movie or TV show, followed by the name of the reviewer.

2▶ Theme Statement

The theme statement tells what the movie or program is about.

3▶ Plot Summary

The summary describes what happens in the movie or program. It should describe the setting or settings, including the time period, and the main characters.

4▶ Critique

In the critique, you give your own opinion of the work, with specifics from the movie or program to support your opinion.

Here are some questions to ask yourself before writing your critique:

- Did you like the movie or TV show? Why or why not?

- Do you feel it was successful as comedy, action-adventure, documentary, drama, fantasy, or horror? Explain.

TIPS

- Were you impressed by the direction, acting, writing, special effects, or some other aspect of the work?

- Would you recommend that a friend see this movie or show?

- Did you learn something from this movie or TV show? Or was its main purpose to entertain?

Reviewing Movies You Liked

- **Don't wait too long**. Most reviewers write their reviews immediately after seeing a movie. This way, the events and characters are still fresh in their minds.

- **Judge the movie on its own terms**. The qualities that make a good action movie are different from those that make a zany comedy or a serious drama. When reviewing any movie, measure it up to other movies of the same kind. Don't try to make it something it isn't.

- **Tell the story in the present tense.** By doing this, you make the movie more exciting for your reader.

- **Critique the movie, not the actors**. Separate the actors from the characters they play. Whether you like a particular actor or not, keep your focus on this movie and the actor's contribution to it.

- **Be balanced in your judgments**. Try to find things you both like and don't like about the movie. A positive review needn't be all positive, nor a negative review all negative.

- **Read a review in a newspaper or magazine to get some ideas.**

Here's a review of a movie the reviewer liked:

The Commitments

by

Ben Felton

The place is Ireland. The time is 1991. The
movie is The Commitments. This was one of the
most wonderful movies that I have ever seen. It
was about this boy who lived in Ireland. He was
eighteen and wanted to start a soul group. In
the beginning you see him walking through the
streets. He goes into a restaurant where there
is a band playing. The bass player and the
guitarist are friends of his. When they are done
playing they go over to him. He tells them about
the idea. (By the way, the kid who wants to
start the band is the manager, so that's what
I'll refer to him as.) The bass player and the
guitarist both think that it is a great idea.
Then when they are talking they see this kid who
is also eighteen (and drunk) get on the stage and
start singing. Although this kid is drunk and
does not know what the heck he is saying, he has
a great voice. This kid turns out to be the lead
singer.

Well, one thing leads to another. The manager
gets a drummer, a sax player, back-up singers,
and a forty-year-old trumpet player. The rest of
the band was eighteen! Well, this guy was really
a kid at heart.

I don't want to tell you every single detail of
the movie, so I'll skip a lot, but I will say one

Dramatic opening

Theme statement

Summary of movie

**Reasons
reviewer
liked it**

thing: the music in this movie was absolutely
terrific. I bought the soundtrack, and it is
great. If the movie did not have the music,
it would not have been as much fun to watch.
The music was one of the many things that
kept me interested.

   This movie was funny, sad, and serious all
at once. The acting was great, and one of
the best things was that the actors were
actually singing and playing the instruments.
Out of five stars, I would give this movie
five stars.

Reviewing Movies You Didn't Like

Here are some pointers to keep in mind when reviewing a
movie you don't like:

- **Give your reasons.** Don't just say the movie is
  terrible, but find specific things in the movie that
  support this opinion.

- **Find something redeeming.** No movie is all bad.
  There must be something in it — a scene, a particular
  actor, or something else — that you like.

- **Admit your prejudices.** Maybe you hate horror
  movies, and if you're reviewing one, you probably
  won't give it a rave review. Tell your readers your
  prejudice, and admit that a person who does like
  horror movies may like this one.

Here is a review of a movie the reviewer didn't like:

```
                    JFK
                    by
                Sam Elliot

    JFK is centered around the New Orleans' district
attorney's investigation of the John F. Kennedy
assassination.  The investigation was  led by Jim
Garrison, who is played by Kevin Costner.  The film
brings up the possibility of a conspiracy and the
probability that Lee Harvey Oswald did not kill the
president.  JFK brings up some intriguing points that
everyone can and should learn from.
    Overall, the movie is shocking!  I was horrified by
the graphic nature of this film.  Oliver Stone
convinced me of the conspiracy theory immediately.
However, I found some scenes to be unnecessary.  In
fact, I thought that all the scenes with Garrison and
his family could have been cut.  Since the film was
three hours long, cutting a few scenes would have
been a big improvement.
    When you see JFK, a word to the wise, don't believe
everything you hear.  This film is not a documentary.
Although it is based on fact, the drama is probably
exaggerated.  You also need to have a little
background on the Kennedy assassination in order to
fully understand the movie.
    I really enjoyed the way the film came together
like a mystery.  Not only will you like the drama of
JFK, but you will learn a lot, too.  Oliver Stone reminds
us that we must continue to search for the truth, and
that we should always protect our rights.
```

Theme statement and brief summary

Reasons reviewer didn't like it

Something redeeming

TV Reviews

A review of a TV show is very similar to a movie review with the following exceptions:

- **If it's a series, watch several episodes.** It's not fair to judge a TV series on the basis of one episode. Watch several episodes to get an idea of who the characters are and what the show is like.

- **If it's a series, don't give a summary of only one episode.** Refer to moments from several episodes of a series. Spend most of the summary giving a description of the main characters, setting, and general tone of the series.

- **Give viewing details.** At the end of your review, let readers know the day, time, and the channel or network where this show can be seen.

 Here is a review of a television series that the reviewer liked:

MacGyver
by
Peter Klein

    MacGyver is about a man (played by Richard Dean) who often ends up in the wrong place at the wrong time, meaning that he usually gets into trouble. Watching him get out of trouble is the best part of the show.

    When he isn't getting into trouble on his own time, he is usually on assignment for the Phoenix Foundation, a government-funded environmental program. MacGyver is also authorized to go on spy adventures. Either way, MacGyver is always chosen for his unique way of getting out of trouble or tight spots. Wherever he is, he uses the laws of science and his surroundings to get out of bad situations.

    I love this show because of the scientific tricks he uses to get out of trouble. It is on channel 7, Mondays at 8 p.m. People who like adventure shows are sure to like MacGyver.

Brief description of main characters and what to expect from the plot

Personal opinion

Viewing information

Appendix

Appendix

State Abbreviations

Use Postal abbreviations on addresses in letters and on envelopes. Use the standard abbreviations for all formal writing.

	Postal	Standard		Postal	Standard
Alabama	AL	Ala.	Montana	MT	Mont.
Alaska	AK	Alaska	Nebraska	NE	Nebr.
Arizona	AZ	Ariz.	Nevada	NV	Nev.
Arkansas	AR	Ark.	New Hampshire	NH	N.H.
California	CA	Calif.	New Jersey	NJ	N.J.
Colorado	CO	Colo.	New Mexico	NM	N.Mex.
Connecticut	CT	Conn.	New York	NY	N.Y.
Delaware	DE	Del.	North Carolina	NC	N.C.
Dist. of Columbia	DC	D.C.	North Dakota	ND	N.Dak.
Florida	FL	Fla.	Ohio	OH	Ohio
Georgia	GA	Ga.	Oklahoma	OK	Okla.
Guam	GU	Guam	Oregon	OR	Oreg.
Hawaii	HI	Hawaii	Pennsylvania	PA	Pa.
Idaho	ID	Idaho	Puerto Rico	PR	P.R.
Illinois	IL	Ill.	Rhode Island	RI	R.I.
Indiana	IN	Ind.	South Carolina	SC	S.C.
Iowa	IA	Iowa	South Dakota	SD	S.Dak.
Kansas	KS	Kans.	Tennessee	TN	Tenn.
Kentucky	KY	Ky.	Texas	TX	Tex.
Louisiana	LA	La.	Utah	UT	Utah
Maine	ME	Maine	Vermont	VT	Vt.
Maryland	MD	Md.	Virginia	VA	Va.
Massachusetts	MA	Mass.	Virgin Islands	VI	V.I.
Michigan	MI	Mich.	Washington	WA	Wash.
Minnesota	MN	Minn.	West Virginia	WV	W.Va.
Mississippi	MS	Miss.	Wisconsin	WI	Wis.
Missouri	MO	Mo.	Wyoming	WY	Wyo.

Where to Write for State Information

Alabama
Bureau of Tourism and Travel
401 Adams Ave.
Montgomery, AL 36103-4309

Alaska
Division of Tourism
P.O. Box # 110801
Juneau, AK 99811

Arizona
Office of Tourism
1100 West Washington
Phoenix, AZ 85007

Arkansas
Dept. of Parks and Tourism
1 Capitol Mall
Little Rock, AR 72201

California
Office of Tourism
Dept. of Commerce
801 K St., Suite 1600
Sacramento, CA 95814

Colorado
Tourism Board
1625 Broadway, Suite 1700
Denver, CO 80202

Connecticut
Tourism Promotion Service
CT Dept. of Economic
Development
865 Brook St.
Rocky Hill, CT 06067-3405

Delaware
Tourism Office
Delaware Development Office
99 Kings Highway
P.O. Box 1401 Dept. RB
Dover, DE 19903

District of Columbia
Washington Convention and
Visitors Association
1212 New York Ave. NW
Washington, DC 20005

Florida
Dept. of Commerce Visitors
Inquiry
126 Van Buren St.
Tallahassee, FL 32399-2000

Georgia
Tourist Division
P.O. Box 1776
Atlanta, GA 30301-1776

Hawaii
Visitors Bureau
2270 Kalakaua Ave., Suite 801
Honolulu, HI 96815

Idaho
Dept. of Commerce
700 W. State St., 2nd Floor
Boise, ID 83720

Illinois
Dept. of Commerce and
Community Affairs
Bureau of Tourism
620 East Adams St.
Springfield, IL 62701

Indiana
Dept. of Commerce,
Tourism and Film Development
Division
One North Capitol
Suite 700
Indianapolis, IN 46204-2288

Iowa
Dept. of Economic Development
Division of Tourism
200 East Grand Avenue
Des Moines, IA 50409

Kansas
Travel and Tourism
Development Division
Dept. of Commerce
400 W. 8th St., 5th Floor
Topeka, KS 66603

Kentucky
Dept. of Travel Development
550 Mero St.
2200 Capital Plaza Tower
Frankfort, KY 40601-1968

Louisiana
Office of Tourism
P.O. Box 94291
Baton Rouge, LA 70804-9291

Maine
Publicity Bureau
97 Winthrop St., P.O. Box 2300
Hallowell, ME 0347-2300

Maryland
Office of Tourism Development
217 E. Redwood St.
Baltimore, MD 21202

Massachusetts
Office of Travel and Tourism
100 Cambridge St., 13th Floor
Boston, MA 02202

Michigan
Travel Bureau
Dept. of Commerce
P.O. Box 30226
Lansing, MI 48909

Minnesota
Office of Tourism
375 Jackson St.
250 Skyway Level
Farm Credit Services Bldg.
St. Paul, MN 55101-1848

Mississippi
Dept. of Economic and
Community Development
Tourism Development
P.O. Box 22825
Jackson, MS 39205-2825

Missouri
Division of Tourism
Truman State Office Bldg.
301 W. High St.
P.O. Box 1055
Jefferson City, MO 65102

Montana
Dept. of Commerce
Travel Montana
1424 9th Avenue
Helena, MT 59620

Nebraska
Dept. of Economic
Development
Division of Travel and Tourism
301 Centennial Mall South
P.O. Box 94666
Lincoln, NE 68509

Nevada
Commission on Tourism
Capitol Complex
Carson City, NV 89710

New Hampshire
Office of Vacation Travel
P.O. Box 856
Concord, NH 03302

New Jersey
Division of Travel and Tourism
CN-826
Trenton, NJ 08625

New Mexico
Dept. of Tourism
Joseph M. Montoya Bldg.
Room 1057
1100 St. Francis Dr.
Santa Fe, NM 87503

New York
Division of Tourism
1 Commerce Plaza
Albany, NY 12245

North Carolina
Travel and Tourism Division
Dept. of Economic and
Community Development
430 North Salisbury St.
Raleigh, NC 27611

North Dakota
Tourism Promotion
Liberty Memorial Bldg.
Capitol Grounds
604 E. Boulevard
Bismarck, ND 58506

Ohio
Division of Travel and
Tourism
P.O. Box 1001
Columbus, OH 43266-0001

Oklahoma
Tourism and Recreation Dept.
Literature Distribution Center
P.O. Box 60000
Oklahoma City, OK 73146

Oregon
Tourism Division Oregon
Economic Development Dept.
775 Summer St. NE
Salem, OR 97310

Pennsylvania
Bureau of Travel Marketing
453 Forum Bldg.
Harrisburg, PA 17120

Rhode Island
Tourism Division
7 Jackson Walkway
Providence, RI 02903

South Carolina
Division of Tourism
P.O. Box 71
Columbia, SC 29202

South Dakota
Dept. of Tourism
Capitol Lake Plaza
Pierre, South Dakota 57501

Tennessee
Dept. of Tourist Development
P.O. Box 23170
Nashville, TN 37202

Texas
Travel Information Services
State Highway Dept.
P.O. Box 5064
Austin, TX 78763-5064

Utah
Travel Council
Council Hall, Capitol Hill
Salt Lake City, UT 84114

Vermont
Agency of Development and
Community Affairs
Travel Division
134 State St.
Montpelier, VT 05602

Virginia
Division of Tourism
1021 East Cary St.
Richmond, VA 23219

Washington
State Dept. of Trade and
Economic Development
101 General Administration
Bldg. AX-13
Olympia, WA 98505-0613

West Virginia
Division of Tourism and Parks
2101 Washington St. E
Charleston, WV 25305

Wisconsin
Dept. of Development
Division of Tourism
Development
P.O. Box 7606
Madison, WI 53707

Wyoming
Division of Tourism
1-25 at College Drive
Cheyenne, WY 82002-0660

Common Editing Symbols

Mark	Meaning	Example
#	new paragraph	# President George Washington was worried.
∧	insert, add this	About two million *people* make their home in the Sahara.
≡	capital letter	Benjamin banneker died in 1806.
/	lower case	The people came in, ate our food, messed up the house, and Left.
ℓ	delete, take out	Parents need to help all teachers plan the school dance.
⊙	add a period	It is the Sahara — the world's largest desert⊙
⤷	move word(s)	We're watching much too TV, and it isn't good for us.
• • • •	stet, let it stay	I recommend it to anyone who likes good westerns.
⌒	close up	If the story so unds familiar, it really is.
#	insert space	The Battleground# is a great show. ∧
∾	transpose	It's on every Thrusday night at 8 p.m.

Using Common Reference Tools

A Dictionary

Use a **dictionary** to look up information about words, such as

- spelling
- history
- use as a part of speech
- pronunciation
- meaning
- other forms

Let's say you want to find out how to spell the word **magnificent** and what it means. Turn to the letter **M** in the dictionary. Guide words at the top of the page will help you find the word within the **M's.** For example, **magnificent** would fall within the guide words **magnet-magnitude.** (Note that **magnificent** and **magnitude** have the same first five letters, but **magnitude's** sixth letter **t** comes after **magnificent's f.**)

Here is a dictionary entry for the word **magnificent:**

word entry   pronunciation   parts of speech

mag • nif • i • cent (mag nif i s nt) adj.
1. presenting a breathtaking appearance; of great beauty   definitions
or splendor. 2. possessing a noble character {Old French magnificent, grand from Latin *magnificientior*, nobler.}—mag•nif• i • cent• ly, adv.

derivation

other form of word

An Encyclopedia

Whether it has one volume or many, an **encyclopedia** has basic information on many topics in alphabetical order. An encyclopedia article, sometimes called an **entry**, is a good way to get an overview of your topic. Here are some tips for using an encyclopedia:

- **Look up your topic under the letter you would expect to find it.** For example, for a report on Atlanta, you would first look in the **A's**.

- **If your topic isn't where you expect to find it, don't give up.** Look in the Index. If the encyclopedia is large, the index may be a separate volume. There you may find that Atlanta is mentioned in an article on State Capitals or one on Georgia.

- **Check the cross-references.** At the end of each article, there is usually a list of other related articles. If you look them up, you may find more information about your topic.

- **Note the copyright date of the encyclopedia**. If you are writing about a science or social studies topic, you want to find out how old the information is. You may want to check another source to find more up-to-date facts. For example, a 1989 encyclopedia will not have the results of the 1990 census.

- **Use the encyclopedia's yearbook**. Most major encyclopedias have a yearbook, a single volume that lists important events and discoveries that happen that year. A yearbook might tell you about the 1996 Olympics in Atlanta.

An Atlas

An atlas is a book that uses maps to organize information. It may simply show location and geographical features, or it may contain information about science, wildlife, population, history, or some other topic.

Here are some features of an atlas that can help you locate information:

- **The Scale.** The scale shows you how to estimate the actual size when using a particular map. For example, on some maps, one inch may represent one mile. On other maps, one inch may represent ten miles. Look for the scale at the bottom or side of a map to help you measure distances.

- **The Key.** The key explains the symbols and colors on a map. For example, a star may indicate a capital city, and a certain color may be used to show all the colonies of a particular nation. Use the key to find out more information.

- **The Index**. The index is an alphabetical listing of the information in the atlas matched to the page number. Sometimes it also gives coordinates, such as C-4. To find the location of the place listed as C-4, you look up the letter C on the edge of the map, and the number 4 at the top or bottom and draw an imaginary line with two fingers to the point where they meet.

- **Charts and Tables**. Additional information such as population figures, elevation above sea level, and distances between cities may be listed in chart form at the back of an atlas.

A Thesaurus

A **thesaurus** is a kind of dictionary that lists words that are similar in meaning to the word you look up (often it also lists words with opposite meanings). Use a thesaurus to look up more interesting words than the one you may have chosen or other ways to state the same idea without repeating yourself. A thesaurus can also help make your writing more specific.

Here is a sample thesaurus entry on the word <u>small</u>:

word entry   parts of speech

small adjective 1. a small person. small things. [informal] baby, compact, concise, diminutive, [informal] dinky, dwarf, exiguous, fractional, infinitesimal, Lilliputian, little, microscopic, minuscule, minute, petite, [informal] pint-sized, pygmy, short, [informal] teeny, tiny toy, undersized, [informal] wee. 2. small helpings. inadequate, insufficient, meager, mean, measly, scanty, stingy 3. a small problem. SEE trivial. OPPOSITES: SEE big.

similar meanings

cross reference

opposite meaning cross reference

Tips on Using a Thesaurus

• **Choose the word that most specifically describes what you are talking about**. For example, you might use the word **small** in a science report to describe bacteria. If you look up **small** in a thesaurus, you might decide that **microscopic** is a more precise way of telling your reader just how small bacteria are.

• **You would want to avoid words marked "informal" in a written report.**

• **Don't get carried away with finding unusual meanings.** Although it can be fun, if you use too many unusual meanings for words, your readers may become confused.

Sources
....

The Reference Department

Reference materials are a good starting place for your research. They will give you a good overview of your topic.

Here are some of the kinds of reference materials you should look at:

- **general encyclopedias** (*The World Book, Collier's Encyclopedia*)

- **specialized encyclopedias** (*Van Nostrand's Scientific Encyclopedia, The Baseball Encyclopedia*)

- **almanacs** (*World Almanac, Information Please Almanac*)

- **other reference works** (*Who's Who, Bartlett's Familiar Quotations, Current Biography*)

The Periodicals Section

Current issues of magazines and newspapers can be found in the periodicals section of the library. For articles on your topic in back issues, look at indices in Reference such as *The Reader's Guide to Periodical Literature* or *The New York Times Index*.

Magazines for kids such as *Super Science Blue, Junior Scholastic, Cobblestone,* and *Faces* often have good material and graphics.

Periodicals often cannot be taken from the library, so be prepared to spend some time there taking notes.

General Circulation

Nonfiction books in general circulation will also deal with your topic. Most of these can be taken home. Here are some of the different types of books you might find useful:

- history books
- true adventure books
- autobiographies
- historical novels
- science books
- biographies
- geography books
- how-to books

- art books

The Computer

Your library may have a computer that is connected to a data base such as Infofinder or ERIC. Once you have decided on a topic, you can use that data base to search for information and a list of sources. The printout can be one of your sources.

Your library may also have CD-ROM disks, such as *Mammals* and the *Guinness Disk of World Records.*

People Sources

People can be valuable sources of information, too. You can interview a person who is an expert on your topic, such as a doctor who treats AIDS patients or a person who has experienced a historic event firsthand, such as a relative who fought or lived through World War II. Make sure you list the person as a source in your report.

Index

Index